# TH
# PRODUCTION
# ASSISTANT'S
# SURVIVAL
# GUIDE

D1628374

Cathie Fraser

Illustrated by

Mark Bernstein

**BBC** *Television Training*

First published in 1990 by
BBC Television Training
BBC Elstree Centre
Clarendon Road
Borehamwood
Hertfordshire

Throughout this booklet the pronoun
'she' should also be taken to refer to
'he'. 'Programme' means any material
gathered for transmission or showing,
from the simplest short item to be
included in a longer programme to a
major documentary.

General Editor: Gordon Croton

Design and production: Shirley Greenfield
Cover photography: John Jefford

Printed by BBC Print Unit,
Evesham, England

# ACKNOWLEDGEMENTS

I would like to thank all those who contributed to the information in this book.

As I mention frequently throughout, you can't be a PA all by yourself — you need help and advice from many other people.

For that reason I have drafted in three PAs expert in their fields to help. My special thanks to:

**Julie Todd** for *Documentary Filming*

**Yvonne Craven** for *Working with Music*

**Kay O'Neill** for *Drama Productions*

# CONTENTS

*Entries in italics denote specimen layouts & check lists*

# PART I

# PART II

# PART III

Crew hours — Film schedule — Distribution — *Film Schedule* — *Shooting schedule* — Clothing — Cash — Packing list — On location — Who says what on location ... — Where to stand — Taking a shot list — Working out the shot sizes — End boards — Mute boards — Good and no good takes — Timing for documentary shoots — Continuity — Entering and leaving frame — Interviews — Crossing the line — Your other roles when on location — There's never enough time — Leave the location tidy — Contributors and back at base — Editec — Live transmissions — *Speedy location (film & OB) checklist — Things to take on location — Foreign locations checklist*

# PART IV

# INTRODUCTION

The job description for production assistants is the longest of all those in the BBC. It begins:

> "The aim of the job is to assist the producer or director in the planning, research, execution and accounting associated with a programme and its supporting materials, by undertaking the detailed administrative work of the office; by being the focal point of reference, liaison and communication throughout the production cycle; by undertaking specialist production duties when filming on location, or OBs, or in the studio; and by providing a high-class secretarial service throughout the production and beyond its duration."

Now if that doesn't put anyone off, nothing will!

It sounds quite a mouthful, but basically it sums up the job pretty well. Anything that needs to be done within the framework of the production, can fall to the PA, and any task that doesn't get done, the PA will probably get blamed for.

You still want to know more ...?

If you are reading this book with a view to becoming a PA, you will find a lot of in-house jargon and much accepted television knowledge. Having read this book you won't be able to say you can do the job, but it will help you to understand the things you will be trained to do once you have become a trainee PA.

If you are a new PA, this should prove a handy reference for situations you haven't come across.

If you are suffering from first day blues in a new office and don't know where to start, I hope this book will help you to survive that initial shock.

For the experienced PA, it might help to jog your memory about things you have forgotten.

The book will be divided into chapters covering all aspects of the PA's work, but you may need to cross reference certain things. There is an expanded contents list at the front, a speedy check list after each specialist programme chapter and a glossary of terms at the back.

Last, but by no means least, I shall acknowledge the PA as female throughout, wishing no discredit to the few men now coming into the profession, but it does still remain a largely female role in production.

# Chapter 1

# The Role of the PA

## PART I

The problem with trying to define the role of the PA and to categorize it, is that the job varies so much depending which company you work for, and even which department within a company. So to lay down the law on the definitive way to do things would be too restricting. The key word must be adaptability.

Many of the jobs expected of a fully trained PA will only arise in certain programme-making areas, so having been through a formal PA training course and learnt all the necessary skills, you may have to store them away somewhere without ever expecting to use them again. But don't be too sure. Many a PA has been caught out thinking that, for example, because they are working in current affairs and doing live galleries all the time, they can forget all they ever knew about drama.

What if the programme decided to re-enact a trial? This would employ all the elements of a full-blown drama, including booking artists, shot calling and continuity.

Time and time again things will crop up which you thought you would never need again and it is hoped that this book will be a useful reference for just that sort of situation. This is particularly true in the freelance world. Small production companies often expect a PA to be also the researcher and the production manager rolled into one. The only problem is that they still only want to pay you as a PA!

Another difficulty nowadays is that a lot of production secretaries are being given the opportunity to act up as PA within a small production company but, unfortunately, do not receive any formal training. They simply pick up the particular skills required for that production, often from an equally ill-trained PA who learnt in the same way, with the result that various 'bad' habits develop. It can also mean that when they wish to move on as a PA, they find they are not well enough equipped to carry the title.

In larger organisations, the PA's status can be under-rated which often discourages some PA's from continuing in the role for any length of time.

It is impossible to draw up a concise A to Z of attributes for a PA, but a few of the essential qualities are: dedication, determination, diligence, diplomacy, dependability, enthusiasm, energy and empathy.

You should also not get discouraged if one aspect of the job just seems to be beyond your command. Many a brilliant drama PA would recoil at the thought of doing a live gallery — and *vice versa*.

You cannot expect to excel at such a wide range of duties which just happen to fall under the one job title. A formal training course will take you through all the skills expected of a PA, and then it is up to you to find your feet and specialise in the area of your choice.

Wherever you find your niche, your role will always involve making everyone's life easier, and this is where many PAs differ in their approach. Some PAs refuse to carry a bag of 'sweeties', thinking that it is not up to them to pander to the sweet tooth of the rest of the production team. Many would recoil in horror at the thought of providing a spare packet of cigarettes for their neurotic director when he runs out. It is a personal choice, but I maintain that if you can help ease the tension in the busy studio gallery or film location, be it with calming words or a tube of mints, then everyone's day will be that much easier.

As a PA you will become a walking stationery cupboard, memory bank and telephone directory, all rolled into one — to say nothing of nursemaid, caretaker, chauffeur, judge and jury, alibi-giver and diplomat. You have been warned!

Knowing the way round a resource facilities office can often be the make or break for a deadline. A negative response to a booking request can often be solved by personal contact and many an experienced PA has learnt the art of renegotiation by by manipulating the system. Not that I am advocating thumping the booking clerk's desk every time your request is turned down, but a symphathetic knowledge of the workings of some of the main servicing departments' allocations systems can often help both sides arrive at a compromise.

Once away from the 'on hand' facilities departments of a large organisation, the PA's role in knowing her way round outside facilities houses is even more crucial. The organisational skills of a PA really come to the fore when she is working on a tight budget, with impossible deadlines. Many companies and freelance production contributors to programmes have individual rules and regulations regarding their terms, so it is very important to establish all the ground rules when booking someone or something.

A lot of the job consists of thinking on your feet and reacting to all sorts of situations. However good you are with office practice, having been a secretary, you'll never make a good PA if you can't think and work on your own initiative. If you can always have 'plan B' up your sleeve, you will have anticipated certain developments which may help to pre-empt a potential disaster.

Lateral thinking seems to help, coupled with a total commitment to the programme you are working on.

# Chapter 2

# A Lightning Guide
# to Who's Who in Television

The titles of the programme and technical staff given below are based on the latest at the BBC. They have changed over the years and will no doubt change again in the future. People are reluctant sometimes to refer to new names, so beware as some people will always be referred to by their old titles.

In the **production gallery,** apart from the producer, director and PA you will normally find:

**The technical co-ordinator** (TC) is the technical administrator of the studio and is in charge of the gallery. He will make sure all your lines of communication and facilities are available, chase any technical problems, communicate with any outside sources on your behalf, run recording VTs and ensure that you don't run into meal breaks or overtime. He will try to negotiate any last-minute requirements for you and attempt to resolve difficulties between production and technical staff which may affect the smooth running of the studio.

All TCs are experienced and knowledgeable and they can help you through almost any problem or crisis. It is the TC who will give permission for guests to be allowed in the gallery.

The **vision mixer** switches pictures and controls some electronic effects. On some long or complex programmes there may be two vision mixers. For complicated effects there may also be a **video effects supervisor**.

In the **sound control room** you will find:

**The sound supervisor** who will mix and monitor the sound for your programme. He will be helped by one or two sound assistants who will operate tape and gramophone machines. There will be other sound assistants on the studio floor dealing directly with all the sound equipment.

In the **lighting/vision control room** you will find:

The **lighting director** (LD) normally lights the production, but on some simple shows it may be the TC operating the lighting control panel.

The **lighting vision control supervisor** (LVCS) works in the lighting control room, operating the dimmers and memorising lighting combinations, whilst the LD is sometimes on the studio floor setting lamps. They are in constant radio contact and if the LD isn't available, then talk to the LVCS.

The **lighting and vision assistant** (LVA)'s job is to control the exposure (lift and gain) of the cameras.

**Studio engineers** help the LVA to 'match' the pictures on cameras by controlling the colour balance of the cameras, slides and sometimes incoming telecine. They are also responsible for 'line- up'.

On the *studio floor* you will find:

**Technical-operations crews** —there are two parts to the tech ops crew — cameras and sound.

The camera crew is led by the **senior cameraman**, who has a deputy and enough crew to operate all the cameras and camera mounts. The camera crew really work direct to the director, but if a dispute arises they are responsible to the TC.

The sound crew is led by the **sound assistant 1**. They operate the booms, rig and move microphones and other sound equipment and help the sound supervisor in the sound control room.

The **floor manager** is responsible for safety and discipline in the studio, ensuring that rehearsals start on time and, as the production progresses, conveying the director's instructions to the artists and everyone else on the studio floor.

On drama and some light entertainment programmes, the floor manager's role will be taken by a production manager.

The **production manager** (PM), like the FM, is in charge of safety and discipline on the studio floor. Ideally he acts as a super organiser planning the scheduling of the production so that the director has no worries about the logistics, such as planning the film schedule and studio recording order.

The **assistant floor manager** (AFM) will have marked up the outside rehearsal room and obtained rehearsal props, attended all outside rehearsals for the show, marked up a fully-blocked script for the director, and will time rehearsals in the absence of the PA. On the studio day the AFM will be responsible for any props used in the action.

The **floor assistant** is in charge of getting artists to the right place at the right time.

The **designer** creates the studio and location sets which are then erected by the scene crew. The designer and assistant will check them and supervise the set dressing by two or three set dressers. There will also be a painter and carpenter available. As the scene crew finish, they hand over to

**production operatives** who make the final adjustments to the set and take over as the rehearsal starts. They move scenery or furniture where necessary and operate any mechanical devices on the floor, such as scoreboards, and help to change captions.

**Make up** — whatever the show, anyone who appears in vision will probably need make-up, so there will be a make-up designer and, depending on the size of the show, a number of make-up assistants.

**Costume** — if there is any costume element in the programme, there will be a costume designer, costume assistants and dressers.

**Dressers** put out and collect costumes and aid actors with complicated costumes or costume changes. They also wash/-clean, dry, iron and repair costumes as required.

**Electricians.** There will be a number of electricians on the studio floor, some setting lamps under the direction of the LD and others connecting up and checking electrical equipment used in the show.

# Chapter 3

# The Production Cycle

Chapter 5 on *Setting up a Programme* will go into the mechanics in greater detail and expand on the subject headings mentioned below, with even further detail contained in each chapter covering specialist programme areas.

But for really new PAs, this lightning guide may help with things encountered during the production cycle.

For this example let us take a six-part weekly magazine programme. It will be a thirty-minute studio-based programme with invited experts and guests, filmed location inserts and an available fact sheet for each programme.

The timescale for setting up this type of programme will vary enormously depending where you are working. The elements that have to be dealt with, though, are as follows:

# PRE-PRODUCTION

### Office administration
- setting up the office
- opening a production file
- finding the production team
- arranging planning meetings
- ordering all the stationery

### Budgeting
- completing a programme budget estimate
- keeping up to date with running costs

### Programme material assembly
- preliminary fact finding, basic research
- preliminary insert material selection
- copyright clearances
- music details

### Artists and contributors
- finding and booking presenters and contributors
- arranging their transport to locations

**Facilities and services**
- booking the studio
- booking the film crew
- booking insert TK machines
- booking TK dub and possible transfer to VT
- booking VT machines
- booking VT sypher dub if required
- liaison with costume and make up-designers
- booking dressing rooms
- organising graphics

**Location arrangements**
- fixing the recce
- typing film schedules
- making hotel arrangements
- making transport arrangements
- booking location catering

**Editing and dubbing film material**

**Transferring material to final format**

**Studio arrangements**
- typing programme scripts and camera cards
- gallery duties
- programme timings

# POST PRODUCTION

**VT editing**

**Sypher dubbing** (not usually required for this type of programme)

**Post production paperwork**

**Programme promotion, presentation and support material**
- liaison with presentation for programme promotion
- transmission documentation

**Type billings and publicity**

**Arrange support material for the programme, leaflets and advice sheets**

**Complete final budget estimate**

**Wrap up correspondence and thank you letters**

Move on to your next production and start all over again!!

# Chapter 4

# Budgeting

Costing a programme is not everyone's favourite part of the job, yet within the context of programme-making it can be an interesting challenge if approached correctly. The degree to which you get involved with the budget will vary considerably depending on what sort of programme you are working on.

### Costing guide/rate card

In most organisations there will be some kind of budget sheet or rate card, itemising all the elements involved in programme budgeting and you simply have to work your way through it and fill in the gaps.

### Budget estimates

Most organisations start with a programme budget estimate (PBE) for each programme, which will be agreed at department, controller or commissioning editor level. From then on, everything you book and use will be charged as cash to your programme. Anything you cancel, close to your production date, may incur a cancellation charge.

### Special rates

Where larger organisations are concerned, there is often an internal cost for certain bookable items and services. Even if you book something late and the service department has to go out of house, the same cost will be charged. However, things are changing and it is advisable to cost everything as a real cash cost for ease of repeat fees and future documentation.

### Programme identification number

Each programme should be issued with a programme identification or costing number and everything for the production will be charged under that code. It will consist of letters and numbers indicating the type of programme, namely self-financed or co-produced, and the originating department, plus a series of core numbers for episodes and a check digit for the computer.

## Costing codes

All the figures and breakdowns of calculations are provided in a specific costing guide, giving each category a code. Armed with this information it really becomes a very straightforward exercise to arrive at a programme budget.

## Keep track of your costings

Costs can tot up very quickly, so keep a close check throughout the production cycle. It is important to know when you are reaching the limit. Break down costings into codes or sections, so when a bill comes in, you can see at a glance how costs are mounting.

If it appears that the programme is going to overspend, warn everyone. If you have an uncaring director, who feels art comes before money, you need to move higher up to the producer or manager.

## Computer printouts

Your manager's office or financial controller will receive reams and reams of computer printouts relating to your programme, so borrow these and check all costs being charged against this number and keep track of the programme budget.

## Convertibility

In a large organisation there is a certain amount of convertibility allowed within a programme budget, but don't be fooled into thinking you can just move money around from code to code and all will be well. It isn't that simple. When in doubt, be sure to ask.

## Strand budgets

If your programme is a long-running magazine programme, you may well have a strand budget for the whole series, in which case it will allow for a little fluctuation between programmes. So, if there is an overspend on one programme and underspend on another, providing the books balance at the end of the series, all will normally be well.

## Allocation of costing for a series

In, for example, a six-part drama series, you are likely to put all your construction costs for sets on to the first programme budget and then allocate the rest of the costs on the budget to which they are directly related. So programme one and programmes two to five in the series will have different totals.

## Producer's final estimate (PFE)

When the programme is complete you will need to do a final budget estimate, accounting for all the money spent for that programme and coding items according to expenditure. This should tally with your initial estimate.

Do be careful when costing items to codes: you may want to cost something for your PFE against a different code to the one it was under in your PBE. Do let your manager know if you want to do this, otherwise the computer will keep throwing up smoke signals that one of your costs has not come in when it is unaware that the item has been costed under a different code.

## Repeats and overseas sales

It is important that your PFE and your PasC (programme as completed) are accurate as they are the most important source of reference for repeats and overseas sales.

## Always check before committing your production

If in doubt about anything concerning costs, your departmental manager will be able to advise you as will the organisers of servicing departments who know their areas intimately.

# Chapter 5

# Setting up a Programme

The setting up of a programme will vary depending on what type of production you are working on, but the basics are very much the same. Each chapter on individual programme types will go into more detail.

## Types of programmes

When you first start as a PA you could find yourself on any kind of programme. Most of the formal training necessitates at least a brief encounter with all programme styles. These will vary from location filming for a documentary to drama. Single-camera video is replacing a lot of film productions now and is certainly used more frequently in current affairs and magazine programmes, whilst much location drama is now shot on video to match in with the studio.

Studio work could include a multi-camera set up, recorded or live. The programmes could be current affairs, chat shows, quiz shows, dramas, magazine programmes. Outside broadcasts could be sports, or staged events, such as ballet, opera or pop concerts — or you could work on large State occasions, such as Royal Weddings and Remembrance Day services. The list is endless and constantly variable, covering the obvious and the unexpected. Once you are fully trained you can specialise.

On day one, if you know nothing about the type of programme you have been assigned to, try to find the departmental manager or producer. Don't sit in the office wondering where to begin. There has probably already been a programme like the one you are starting, so go and find out how it was set up. The PA from that programme may still be around to consult, or the production files may be to hand. Very little in the broadcasting field is so original that there isn't some previous material to help get you started.

As the PA is usually the first of the production team to arrive, there may well be the chance of some peace and quiet before the rest of the team turn up to organise a system. It's then *your* system and you know it will work. Don't however, make it so exclusive that no one else can find their way round it. The production system that you set up is available to everyone on the team.

## The production file

As soon as you can, start a production file. As information comes in, it can then be organised into your system. Every PA tackles setting up a production file in a different way, but the contents of the programme will very much dictate what sections you will need for a logical file.

The most common sections for any type of programme would be:

- Costing
- Artists/contributors
- Studio arrangements
- Filming
- Bookings
- Correspondence

As soon as you have set up a production file, get things sorted out as soon as possible — it will help as a reminder of when everything needs to be ordered. Once you are into the production, information will be pouring in from all directions, and it is important that you know how to find anything at a moment's notice. You are, after all, going to be the focal point of reference and communication throughout the production.

## Getting organised

Organisation is such a key word for a successful PA — and so many simple little things make life easier.

Use a hardback notebook, rather than a shorthand notebook, which may well innocently get 'borrowed' from your desk with the result that the information has gone forever. It also lasts longer, hopefully right to the end of one production cycle, so that the vital 'phone number, scribbled down weeks ago, is somewhere in there when you desperately need it, rather than in one of six notepads or on the back of last week's script.

With any job, planning is important to ensure the smooth running of the production, and the more you can plan at an early stage, the calmer and happier your production will be.

### Contacts

Once you know what sort of programme you are working on, you should be able to start finding out who will be servicing your programme.

Some PAs produce wall charts, so that important dates and names are seen at a glance by anyone in the office; this tends to happen mainly in larger drama productions, and will be covered in greater detail in Chapter 16.

### Address book

It is vital for an organised PA to have all the regularly-used telephone numbers on the tip of her tongue. With constant use, most numbers are quickly remembered, but do have an address book — and keep it with you wherever you go. Get the home telephone numbers of your immediate production team, as well as the key technical contributors, in case there are late important changes.

List telephone numbers such as: reception, security gate, VT and TK controls, programme transport department, local taxi companies, resource departments — main numbers and specialist numbers, other useful planning departments, key servicing departments' main offices, contracts department, copyright department, local police station, local hospital, canteens and crush bars (with opening times noted).

The list can be endless, but your address book will prove one of the most useful things you can compile.

### Stationery

Order enough stationery to last throughout your production: some departments have easy access to a supply, but others rely on special orders, which can take time. So make sure you never run out, especially if you are going to be working away from base.

### Planning meetings

You will need to organise planning meetings, find the people involved and arrange a convenient time; take notes of what was said and agreed, and act on anything where appropriate.

### The budget

There may already be a budget agreed for the programme or you may find you and the producer/director have to do one. It is the PA's responsibility, once a budget has been agreed, to keep a running total of expenditure. It is, however, important to stress that it is the producer's inescapable responsibility to keep within budget, and you can only do your best to advise everyone where the possiblities of an overspend may occur.

### Deadlines

Certain aspects of the programme might have already been agreed by the time you join the production, such as location or studio elements. Dates and times may well already be in the schedules, so plan a skeleton production timetable as you already have deadlines to meet. As soon as possible let those involved know any dates that need concern them, by working back from transmission date.

### Facilities

The PA will need to book the facilities required for the programme. If there is no statutory production office paperwork system, I would always recommend confirming telephone bookings in writing. It saves a lot of worry when facilities don't appear as expected.

Start booking facilities early. At least make the facilities departments aware of your needs and timescale, even if precise dates and times are not available at this stage. They can then at least begin to allocate facilities.

# The Production Cycle

## SET UP A PROGRAMME FILE

| COSTING | ADMIN | FILMING | STUDIO | POST PROD. |
|---------|-------|---------|--------|------------|
| BUDGET ESTIMATE | PROGRAMME RESEARCH | LOCATION RESEARCH | STUDIO SET UP | PICTORIAL PUBLICITY |
| | COMMISSION MUSIC | RECCE | BOOKING RESOURCES | |
| MONITOR COSTS | COPYRIGHT CLEARANCES | TYPE SCHEDULE | PLANNING MEETINGS | |
| | CASTING | BOOKING LOCATIONS | BOOK GRAPHICS | PROGRAMME SUPPORT MATERIAL |
| | ARTISTS CONTRACTS | HOTEL BOOKINGS | SCRIPT & CAM. CARDS | |
| | ACQUISITION OF FOOTAGE | CATERING ARRANGEMENTS | RECORDING ORDER | |
| | | | TECH RUN | |
| | | FILMING | STUDIO RECORDING | |
| | ARTISTS' TIME SHEETS | EDITING | OFF LINE EDIT | BILLINGS |
| | | FILM DUB | VT EDITING | THANK YOU LETTERS |
| | | TRANSFER | SYPHER | TX FORMS |
| FINAL COSTS | CLEAR UP OFFICE | | | FILING |

Work out as much as you can as early as you can. If you have booked things very early, there is no harm in checking nearer the production date that everything is correct.

As I mentioned in the initial introduction, the PA's role covers just about everything and anything. Listed below are a number of other tasks you may find yourself involved with.

## Co-productions

More and more companies are entering into co-production deals in order to be able to produce the more expensive types of programmes, such as costume dramas, music extravaganzas and the larger sporting events.

There are a number of strict rules governing co-productions and failure to comply with relevant procedures may not only be expensive, but also time consuming. In some cases, failure to deliver material to co-producers on time can be deemed to be a breach of contract.

It is essential that all music, stills, film clips, etc. are cleared for world use. It will be necessary to split the sound tracks of your final programme to allow for foreign language versions to be dubbed.

Your PasC and post production transcript will form a very important part of the contractual material connected with the co-production.

## Programme research

Many PAs feel that research is not part of their duties. However, basic research is expected of a PA and can, in most cases, enhance the interest of the programme you are working on. Sometimes it will only involve initial skills research at libraries or organisations, but on occasions can involve location finding and more in-depth information research.

It is also important to keep copyright department informed, so that the appropriate permissions can be sought; it will also act as an early warning if there are any unforeseen problems concerning copyright.

There may also be a call for some research into music composition or usage. Many libraries and specialists can help you in this area, and you should again be aware of any copyright problems.

## Location research

If working on a drama, you may well get involved in finding locations for filming. Some large organisations have a department dedicated to keeping track of locations which have proved useful in the past.

## Sub-titles

If your programme is either for the deaf, an opera or for sale abroad, you may have to get involved with sub-titling. This usually means getting a VHS copy with time code, which can be transferred on to a floppy disc containing the sub-titles timed to the time code.

## Proof reader

You may well have to proof read the sub-titles or any graphics for inclusion in the programme. Check spellings of guests' names and details ... mistakes are time wasting and expensive.

## Forward planner/runner on location

It may be appropriate for you not to do a shot list on one particular programme, because the time would be better spent fixing up the next location or finding the next interviewee.

## Public relations

Many studio programmes have a hospitality suite arranged to welcome their guests prior to the programme. It often falls to the PA to check that everyone is happy and pour out the occasional glass of wine.

## Marking up stills

You may find the programme requires some benchwork or rostrum camera work carried out on stills. This is where stills pictures can be recorded on either film or video and be given some movement. They are mostly used for illustration within a documentary programme, where they will cover the commentary.

A rostrum camera expert can help you with the type of movements best suited to the picture and advise on the speed of the movement.

The best way to present work for rostrum camera is with a start and finish position clearly marked on a covering of tracing paper. For example, the marked up diagram below requires an opening shot (position A) to be held for ten seconds, then a five-second zoom out to position B and that is held for ten seconds.

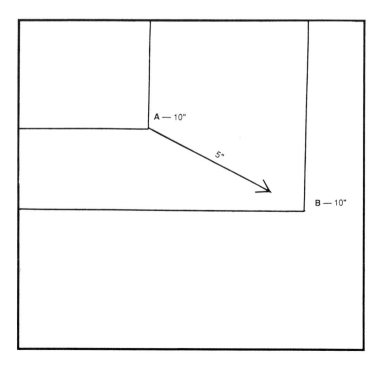

## Checklists

It is often useful to make a checklist of jobs that need to be done within your programme cycle, so that there is something to refer to when the pressure is on. Each programme chapter in this book ends with a 'speedy checklist' for reference.

Every programme will demand different skills from its PA, but if you can prepare well and make sure all the production team plan well, you should be *en route* towards a successful production.

Remember that telepathy is not all that high on anyone's list of qualities, although many expect it of a PA. Be everyone's eyes and ears and the answer to everyone's prayers all rolled into one and you can't go far wrong!

# Chapter 6

# Production Paperwork & Office Procedures

The paperwork is the bit no one ever wants to do. But it is essential and it is also very important to keep up-to-date. Even in the most hectic production, the paperwork is vital to ensure that all the bookings arrive on time, that contributors get paid, and that the programme goes out on air as planned.

I don't want to go into too much detail about specific production office paperwork systems as all companies have different ways of doing things. In small production companies it is usually up to the PA to devise a system.

In larger organisations, formal production office paperwork systems are colour coded for easy retrieval in a production file. All the forms ask the necessary questions, so you just fill in the gaps and await results. There is also the facility for a copy of the form to be returned as confirmation of the booking.

All these things contribute greatly to getting the correct facilities when and where you want them. So, before the production has any chance of getting produced, there will be a million-and-one things to be arranged and ordered.

It is important to book early. Certain departments have set dates (or zero dates) ahead of recording or transmission when bookings have to be made. Likewise there is usually a penalty for late cancellation or misuse of a facility or resource.

Once you know the elements of your programme, and whether it is on film or videotape, certain things fall into line.

It is usually impossible to get full details of all requirements until you are well into production. But if you can begin to see what your needs are, it all helps to build a framework for the production and gives the servicing departments an idea of loading.

Do remember at this stage that there is always an expert somewhere who can advise on which bit of equipment is best for your requirements, and always another PA or departmental manager who can advise in the absence of the producer or director.

### Where do you start?... questions to ask

- If your programme is entirely on film, is it to be transmitted as such or transferred to video? More and more organisations no longer transmit on film, so a transfer is essential.

- If on video, which video format?

- Do you need insert machines for your studio recording?

- Does your film need a dub?

- Does your final video need a sypher dub?

- How much editing does your programme need?

- Do you need specially composed music?

- Are there any special dietary requirements for foreign guests on your programme?

- Do any animals need special facilities?

- What is your graphics requirement?

- Will you want rostrum camera work?

- If you are working on an OB, will you be recording on site or back at base?

- What travel arrangements need to be made?

- Are there any safety requirements for hazardous substances in the studio or firearms?

- Do you need audience tickets designed?

- Do you need insurance for valuables in the studio or on location?

- Will you need special effects equipment and an operator?

And so on. Don't panic, the first thousand questions are usually the worst!! But at least you now have a flavour of the sorts of questions you need to ask as you set up a programme and start to plan the production.

You may be well into production as things finally fall into place, but keep on thinking ahead and try to anticipate any potential problems.

The technical side of a programme can sometimes get a bit confusing for new PAs, but there will usually be an expert somewhere to help you make sure you order the right piece of equipment to do the job properly. There is also the danger of a director wanting the biggest whizz-bang piece of machinery he can find when he actually needs the simplest of effects. He could finally order something that might not even do the simple job he requires and will certainly cause the production unnecessary expense and deny another production the equipment that it really needs.

Don't be afraid to seek advice in specialist areas before falling into the trap of simply ordering everything your possibly over-zealous director has requested.

Try not to leave things until the last moment: late bookings are not always possible and can prove costly. Don't let your director prevaricate and delay his decisions. Artists and machinery are not a constantly obtainable commodity.

Once the production is over, don't for a moment think you can relax and enjoy yourself: another task lies ahead of you — the headache of all the post-production paperwork, which is covered fully in a later chapter.

# Chapter 7

# Copyright & Contracts

## Copyright

Broadly speaking, copyright is the protection given by law to an author for his work — the word 'author' also covers artists (in the sense of painters and sculptors), composers, architects, photographers, choreographers, etc. The 'works' created by these people are obvious — stories, plays, poems, photographs, musical compositions, ballets, paintings, statues, buildings.

But there are also other classes of people who are given a different kind of copyright protection; thus a gramophone record manufacturer or the maker of a film has a copyright in his record or film quite distinct from the work recorded or filmed, and a broadcasting organisation, such as the BBC or the IBA has a copyright in its broadcast quite distinct from the works included in the broadcast.

Generally speaking, copyright owners have the sole right to use or authorise the use of the works in which they own copyright, although there are certain uses which may be made of copyright works which do not constitute an infringement of the copyright. For example, if you buy a book, you can hire it or sell it, but you are not entitled to photocopy it, or broadcast extracts from it, without the author's permission.

The conditions for obtaining copyright are far too complicated to go into in this book and should always be left to the experts. All you need to remember is that if you can see it or hear it, then you have probably got to pay for it! You may be lucky and find there will be no fee involved, but the use of the work will still need to be cleared for copyright and a contract drawn up indicating the agreement.

Always seek advice and never accept anyone saying "Oh, I'm sure it'll be all right". If you haven't cleared the copyright of something prior to transmission, you really don't have a leg to stand on afterwards, when the copyright owner comes forward. Copyright department or a copyright expert will advise you on all aspects of clearance of any bought-in footage and music for UK or world rights.

## Music copyright

One of the most complex areas of copyright is that of music. It is essential that you are accurate when timing music for your post-production paperwork.

There are three main organisations which will need details of music in a programme:

*The Performing Rights Society* (P.R.S.) is the society that looks after the interests of the composers and performers of all music which is performed and broadcast.

*The Mechanical Copyright Protection Society* (M.C.P.S.) is the society which protects all recorded music.

*Phonographic Performance Ltd* (P.P.L.) receives an annual lump sum to cover the dubbing of commercial gramophone records for direct broadcasting.

Generally, broadcast companies pay a lump sum to the *Performing Rights Society* to cover the use of published music and a good deal of manuscript music. There is a very small number of composers who are not members of the P.R.S. and so their work is not covered. Nearly all of this work is unpublished. This blanket payment does make the PA's job considerably easier, but it still means it is essential that you report all music used on the programme as completed form, under the music section.

Dramatico-musical works, such as operas, musical plays, ballet, etc do not come under the *Performing Rights Society*, so they have to be cleared separately.

Gramophone libraries in large organisations usually only keep records that are cleared for UK transmission. However, special clearance may be needed for programmes being sold abroad.

Recorded music obtained from other sources will need to be checked as they may not even be cleared for UK transmission.

Always check with your music copyright department for any details of the agreements as there are literally hundreds of clauses to cover all needs.

Remember that people who are entitled to fees will not get paid unless your information is complete and accurate. These will include not only the composer and performers, but also people like the arranger.

You must endeavour to find out the details of all music used in your programme and be as thorough as possible — the tune the window cleaner was whistling, the music the band was playing in the street, the song the pianist was singing in the pub, all of them must be reported along with the duration, no matter how short.

### Acquisition of footage for programme use

Very few productions record or shoot all the material required for a programme and it is therefore necessary to buy-in footage from outside sources. This could be archive material, special events or news footage and it is essential to do your research and check on distributors and copyright holders.

An **acquisitions clerk** will check availability for you, any copyright clearance problems and the likely cost of such clearances. They will also make arrangements for films to be made available for viewing, but do remember that until copyright clearance has been arranged no footage from an outside source may be copied for inclusion into a programme.

Following a request for clearance of footage, an assistant will negotiate with the supplier concerned and will issue a contract (known as a *Sequence Licence Agreement or SLA)* to the supplier confirming the rate agreed for the film. Copies are then sent to the production.

As soon as the programme has been completed and the exact footage included in the programme is known, inform the acquisitions clerk of the details so that payment to the supplier can be authorised.

# CONTRACTS

As with many areas within the scope of the PA's role, this is one you should have an outline comprehension of, but in no way should you tackle contracts directly.

For the purposes of booking artists, each programme area within a large organisation should have an artist booker who will deal with all artists and agents, negotiate contracts and discuss money. In a smaller production company let the producer negotiate the price.

Your role within a production when artists are being booked will involve ringing agents and checking their availability. However, NEVER attempt even to suggest a possible fee to an artist's agent who may well use your suggestion as a starting point for negotiations.

Certain fee levels are set with Union agreements and large organisations may well have an artist index, giving details about all artists and presenters used, which productions can refer to regarding fee levels prior to approach.

The precise details of all the Union agreements will change from time to time, so if you need to read through the whole document to check anything for a booking, don't trust that information as gospel for evermore.

There are hundreds of clauses for length of rehearsal times, overtime rates, repeat fees, etc. When booking any performers, it is important to book them as accurately as possible from the start, otherwise extra costs may be incurred when changes are made. Do keep your artists' booker up to date on every decision affecting artists.

If you are going to work on, let us say, a long and complex music programme, you would be well served by reading the MU and ISM agreements before starting. The rules and regulations governing musicians are extremely complicated. Strict rules govern rehearsal times, doubling, performance schedules, overtime rates, etc. It is also vital when working out details with the booker that the use of the music is taken into account, especially when sessions are for, say, incidental music for a six-part series. Before each session, therefore, you must be sure in which episode each piece of music will be used.

## Equity

Equity is the Union for actors and actresses, light entertainment and variety artists, choreographers, stunt men and arrangers, chorus singers, puppeteers, opera and ballet artists, stage managers, supporting artists and walk-ons.

## Supplementary payments

Any supplementary payments due to artists for overtime, additional rehearsals or recordings, wardrobe calls, haircuts, etc must be notified to the artist booker as soon as possible — usually on a weekly basis for longer productions.

## Musicians Union (MU)

Orchestral musicians, chamber musicians, pop groups (where the make up of the group is predominantly instrumental), music directors, rehearsal pianists, all belong to the MU.

## Incorporated Society of Musicians (ISM)

The ISM covers instrumental and vocal soloists (except principals in opera and solo light entertainment singers), symphonic and concert orchestral conductors, opera and ballet conductors, accompanists and church musicians.

## Long-term contracts

Many presenters on magazine strands, news and current affairs programmes will come under this bracket. Use of a presenter under a long-term contract by another department would need the approval of the Head of Department responsible for the contract. Permission may also be given to undertake a certain amount of freelance work.

## Foreign artists

Foreign artists from non-EEC countries invited to work in the U.K. require a work permit. Artists possessing a permit for, say, a concert tour may not be eligible to work in television and will need further authorisation for such work. The Department of Employment require at least six weeks to process permit applications.

## Co-productions

It is essential that contracts issued for co-produced programmes should reflect the rights granted to the co-producer. Production offices must inform their contracts department if the programme is to be co-produced at the earliest possible moment, stating what rights have been granted to the co-producer.

## Short extracts from past programmes

Under the terms of union agreements, limited use is allowed in certain programme categories only, for a small fee or donation. Extracts of performances contracted on Equity type contracts require special clearance if the programme from which the extract is taken is more than four years old.

## Obituaries

Most rules will be waived in the case of a short news obituary item, providing only short clips are used, but for a lengthier reflective programme obituary, the usual rules are likely to apply.

## Location facilities

Locations should be formally contracted for use in programme making, as this is essential for insurance purposes. Like artists, larger organisations will keep a list of all previously used locations with costs and any relevant details. Refer to the list for a guide to fee levels, but again, don't talk money direct — leave it to the facilities booker to arrange.

## No fee

Even if no fee is required for either the artist's performance or location, it is still vital that a contract is drawn up. This then provides copyright in the material, and provides the owner with flexibility to edit recorded footage. The form used for this is a **facility form** when either a cash payment or an agreement for no fee is made for either appearance or use of facilities. The contributor's signature ensures copyright and they have a receipt as their part of the contract.

## Children

Children up to the legal school leaving age are subject to strict controls on working hours. Almost without exception a Licence from the child's local authority is necessary. Chaperones and tutors may also be required. Consent of head teachers and parents or guardians is essential.

I had hoped to devise an 'at-a-glance' guide which would show the complexities of using children in a production, but as things change so rapidly it seemed more appropriate to summarise the problem areas and to remind you to check with an expert.

The things to watch out for are the times certain age groups can be rehearsed and recorded. For instance, children under five can only work for up to thirty minutes at a stretch and only between certain hours of the day. For any children, you will have to build the appropriate rest and homework periods into the schedule.

If the regulations prove too restricting for the rest of the production, some directors will go to enormous lengths to shoot round the scene with the baby in the pram, so you can get away with sound effects and never see the screaming baby.

One final point, remember it is the actor's age that matters, not the character's age, so if you can find an over-sixteen year old who looks under sixteen, then use them.

# Chapter 8

# The PA's Role in Post Production

# PART II

Having spent weeks, often months, setting up a programme, working towards the hectic days on location and in the studio, you now need to begin the task of assembling the raw material ready for the great viewing public.

Many of the production team move on at this stage leaving you and the director with a new team of post-production experts to help you complete the programme.

You have pages and pages of continuity notes, shot lists, time code notes and lots of spool numbers — so what next?

The following is a brief outline of processes connected with post production with which the PA may be involved — more detail can be found in the specialist chapters.

**Film editing**

Once back from the laboratories, the film rushes will go to the film editor who will cut them together using your notes (e.g. the shot list) and any other information provided by the programme director.

Film is a flexible editing medium, so changes can easily be made, but the patience of many an editor has been worn thin by a director who constantly changes his mind.

You should also be aware of any continuity problems arising out of changes which take place in the cutting room.

**Film dubbing**

The film editor will track lay all the different tracks of sound required for the sound dub, be it dialogue, music or sound effects (see dubbing sheet on p.134).

For a normal dub there is usually little the PA needs to do, unless there is to be a commentary dub, in which case you will need to type a dubbing script, noting all the sound cues for the commentator or presenter (see the example of a commentary script on p.135).

## Off-line editing

Using your notes in a re-vamped readable form, together with a VHS copy of the recording, the director can do a rough cut edit on VHS before the main editing session.

The burnt-in time code will enable you to check an overall timing and adjustments made prior to the final edit.

## VT editing

Unlike film, VT editors start with frame one and work through the programme, unable to leave gaps for flexible editing. To re-edit many times loses generations and degrades the quality of the pictures, so precise notes are essential, along with a clear idea of what you want.

When organisations change to digital tape (D2) degradation will not occur but, for the time being, assume that the existing type of tape is being used and therefore generation loss might be a problem.

## Sypher

This stands for Synchronized Post dub Helical scan Eight track Recorder! It is the VT equivalent to film dubbing and is mainly used for music productions or drama. The original sound is lifted off the VT tape on to an eight-track tape recorder, re-mixed and then put back on to the original tape using time code as a guide track.

It requires a variety of processes of dubbing on to U-matic with time code for the re-mix. Don't forget all the extra tape costs when budgeting for a sypher dub.

## Incidental music recordings

You may find yourself involved in arranging sessions for incidental music recordings following your programme edit. These may involve a revised script with timings on for the composer to work to.

# POST PRODUCTION PAPERWORK

After the production you are invariably the last to leave and have to cope with all the post-production paperwork and thank you letters.

### Programme-as-completed

The PasC is the only written record of the contents of a programme. It provides all the information to fulfil financial and legal obligations to contributors. It is also an essential reference for repeat transmissions, detailing any contractual limitations. It outlines the nature and content of the programme including all contributors, gives sources of all insert material and records all the music content.

### Post production script

This is an accurate record of the final edited programme which, coupled with your PasC, provides an accurate record of the programme as it was transmitted and contains details of all bought-in footage used in the programme.

### Copyright details

Make sure that all copyright details are noted and all passed on to the appropriate department or person so that copyright payments can be made.

### Music returns

List all the music contained in the programme, using the appropriate form.

### Artists payments

You must make sure that all payments have gone through the contracts department, otherwise many artists may find themselves waiting months for payment if the paperwork doesn't go through promptly.

### Final costs / producer's final estimate

An accurate record of all production costs as spent. If this is computerised, do make sure that the items listed match the codes from the initial budget estimate and send copies to all appropriate places.

### Billings

Billings will be required for the programme, publicity information and possibly photographs: all these things can be handed over to the manager's office if the programme is not due for transmission for some time.

### Publicity

Publicity is usually dealt with through a Press Office or the departmental manager. Liaison regarding photos or publicity material should be timed to coincide with transmission.

### Transmission paperwork

Once the programme is completed and ready for transmission, presentation will need all the details including copies of the final script. Larger organisations have a specific form for all the necessary details, which usually include:

- Precise details of the programme content, in case of sensitivities at the time of transmission.

- Precise details of the opening and closing of the programme, to ensure that it gets on and off air smoothly.

- Duration of the closing credits, in case a trail is run off the back of the programme.

- Any information required by the announcer to introduce or pay-off the programme.

Various other offices also require final copies of the script, such as script library and the duty office for viewers' enquiries.

### Repeat transmission paperwork

If the programme is to be repeated, paperwork will be required to ensure payments are made. This will be based on information you have supplied on the first transmission, so it is essential that it is complete and correct.

Don't just copy the first transmission form. Details on that may only apply for the first showing, such as an exhibition or publication connected with the programme.

### Thank you letters

You need to write thank you letters to those who helped the production, including both outside contributors and service department staff. You never know when you may need them again!!

### When it's all over

Before you leave the production office for the last time, make sure the departmental manager has all the relevant paperwork, the appropriate library has your filing and that you have left the office in the state you would like to find it.

Make sure all the charts are off the wall and the cupboards cleared of any unwanted programme material. Just to be on the safe side, leave the new occupants with a list of forwarding telephone numbers and addresses for your team. Calls seem to come in for months after the production has folded.

There is always a danger that everyone disappears too quickly after a production, and you may well find you are chasing information for one programme whilst setting up the next, but it is important that a programme is completed correctly and that task always falls to the PA..

# Chapter 9

# The PA's Role in the Gallery

Each type of programme will demand different things of the PA. In this chapter I will describe the PA's role in the gallery, although more detail will appear within each programme chapter and under specialist headings.

### First to arrive, last to leave

- Arrive early, meet the crew, get their names for the director and distribute scripts and camera cards to the floor.

- Distribute scripts to all the contributing sources for your programme. VT and TK play-in machine operators, reception, etc.

- Check captions and slides and take them to the appropriate places, loading them if required.

- Check with caption generator operator that all supers are correctly spelt and in programme style and colour.

- Give floor manager spare scripts and running orders and explain any potential difficulties.

- Check arrangements for visitors with reception, especially VIPs. Has a hospitality room been booked? Has the door been unlocked? Has the hospitality trolley arrived with the correct items on it?

- Check you have everything up to date, and make sure all the essential people have got the script changes.

- Check the desk stopwatch and, along with your portable ones, wind them all up.

- Check the clock time with the speaking clock, if required for on-air time.

- Be ready in the gallery promptly for the start of rehearsals.

- If the director breaks off rehearsal for any reason, make sure the floor knows what is happening.

**Keeping on schedule**

Have a rough idea when rehearsals start and what stage you should have reached at any given time. You can then warn the director, if things are taking longer than expected.

---

**Things to take to the gallery for recording or transmission**

Scripts
Separate running orders
Camera cards and spares
Captions/graphics
Slides
Discs/tapes etc. for sound
Telephone directories (internal if appropriate)
List of contact numbers for staff and artists
Notebook
Paper
Biros and/or felt pens (several colours and spares)
Pencils
Rubber
Ruler
Sellotape
Paper clips
Stapler and staples
Scissors
Production file

*from here on its up to you...*

Paracetamol
Handkerchiefs
Matches
Sweets
Spare cigarettes (if smoking is permitted in the gallery)

## Meal breaks

You must stick to the schedule provided for your studio day. If a director wants to over-run into a meal break it is important to request permission from the technical co-ordinator and senior cameraman. Any late start to a meal break, must be transferred to a late return by the same amount.

## Previewing

Always preview camera sources before calling shots so that you can double check that the shot is correct and that the boom is out of view. You should also check that all incoming sources are correct and on cue.

## Communicating in the gallery

As most of the sources into your programme will be somewhere other than in the production gallery, you need to talk to them over 'talkback'.

## Open talkback

Once switched on, everything said in the gallery will be heard by all the incoming sources to your studio; VT, TK, graphics input area, etc and can even be picked up through a ringmain system, if required, in offices — so do be careful what you say. Your words may travel further than you wish.

Be particularly wary of reporters or guests who have a feed on an earpiece in a remote studio, as they usually have gallery talkback for sound checks until this is switched to programme sound.

On most sports, news and current affairs programmes, the presenters will stay on open talkback, hearing everything through their earpiece during the programme. It is a skill few presenters choose as they are filtering so much gallery noise whilst trying to appear calm in front of the camera. It means the production team must be disciplined in the gallery and curb any unnecessary chatter during recordings and transmission.

## Switched talkback

This is used as the link to the presenter. You and the director will have switches on the production desk which will open a circuit to the presenter's earpiece. If you are giving instructions through switched talkback, they will hear nothing unless the switch is engaged.

It does mean that on a busy programme, the presenter does not have to hear everything from the gallery, but only selected information. It is therefore important, prior to the recording or transmission, that you check your talkback to the presenters. They could be on one talkback each or share one feed. If they do, be careful when you talk to one presenter, if the other is reading a script at the time. Precede your chat by the relevant presenter's name, because it saves them both listening, when the information is only of use to one.

When giving timings in the gallery, try to pick a good moment for the presenter. During an interview, for example, wait until he or she is listening to an answer before giving timings, and adjust accordingly. Far better to say "just under two minutes left on this interview" than interrupt to give a precise time check.

If you are talking over switched-talkback to a presenter, try to look at the monitor they are on, so that if they look as if they didn't hear the information properly, you can repeat it.

## Communicating with insert machine operators

VT and TK insert machines are rarely anywhere near the studio gallery, so when you speak to the operator over talkback, he will respond in a variety of ways depending on the studio. The recognised responses can either be a series of buzzes, a flick of the 'comms' button or a flash of picture on the gallery monitor.

If he is using buzzes, the rules are very simple — one buzz means 'yes', two buzzes mean 'no'. It is also good if you can acknowledge his response.

It is surprising what an interesting conversation you can have with a machine in a quieter moment, when they can only respond with a buzz!

It may sound strange, but look at the source that you are talking to. So, as you ask a VT machine operator to stand by, look up at the monitor. If you don't get a response but see the machine frantically spooling to the next clip, you could ask for a long buzz or suitable response once the insert is on cue, or at least know the reason why you haven't had a response.

### Tunnel hearing and spreadeagle vision

You need to be able to concentrate on certain things and shut out such distractions as the argument that could be going on in the back of the gallery.

You also need to be able to keep an eye on everything, be it VT sources with correct idents for the next inject or outside sources ready for insertion into the programme, whilst having an eye on transmission and any other factors which might affect your programme, such as the outputs of the caption generator and stills store. If you are expecting an inject from a region, keep an eye on the monitor to check the source is there. Is it a reporter piece and are they ready for their inject?

### Telephone

The telephone should not ring in a gallery once it is in rehearse or record mode, but a light should flash to indicate a call. You should answer the 'phone during rehearsals, but your technical co-ordinator can take over during recording or transmission. It is, however, important that it is not ignored, especially during a live current affairs or news programme. It could contain vital information for the programme.

### Marking up your script

Try to start off in pencil. There could be lots of changes and too many alterations could lead to problems later. Once everything has been finalised, and before recording or transmission, outline the important things. Mark them in colour, and check that you rub out items which are no longer relevant.

Check on the implications of changes to a script. You may find that, having dropped one clip, a camera will no longer have time to get from one shot to another.

Try to check all the script alterations with the vision mixer, so you are all doing the same thing. Some cameramen appreciate a new camera card if the changes are considerable, but do check with him before taking all his notes in order to re-type the card.

## Marking stand-bys and run cues for TK and VT machines

Find out the programme style for run cues. Certain programmes follow certain styles. News tend to run everything off a standard cue, regardless of what format the insert is on. This could either be a three-second or five-second cue.

Other programmes have a ten-second run cue for opening titles, with everything else on a five-second cue. Film inserts tend to have an eight-second run cue, showing a 'ten' in the gate; some PAs like to alter this to a 'twelve' in the gate for a ten-second run cue.

However, be warned — different TK machines run up at different speeds, newer machines take less time to run up. Check with the technical co-ordinator and the TK machine operator, then make sure everyone who needs to know, knows what you are going to do.

## Working out run cues

The average spoken word speed for presenters is three words a second. So if you are working out a five-second run cue, count back fifteen words from the point you wish the insert to appear. Some presenters vary, so once you have worked with someone for a while you can make the necessary adjustments. Don't get caught out by common traps in scripts; allow time for long foreign place names, lists of things — dates catch many PAs out; 1991 looks like one word until you say it — "nineteen ninety-one". Information covered by animated graphics sequences will also read slower, so allow enough time.

Make allowances for a breath between sentences or for a reaction prior to the insert appearing. A bad news story might be read at a slower pace than a good news story, so do allow for the mood of the text.

Marking stand-bys and run cues should be done initially in pencil, to allow for changes but, once confirmed, outline in a strong colour so that they won't be missed.

## Stand-bys

You should stand-by all insert machines, approximately thirty seconds before running them. If that is in an awkward place, let the machine know that the stand-by is at a different time, i.e. 'long stand-by'.

When using more than one insert machine, stand-by the machine number. Wait for a response from each machine, before standing by the next, and stand them by in the order they appear in the programme.

If you can also identify the insert as well as stating the machine number it makes things that much clearer.

For example:

"Stand-by VT6 with opening titles". (Wait for BUZZ response)
"Stand-by VT3 with 'Housing' tease". (Wait for BUZZ response)
"Long stand-by VT26 with 'Dogs' tease". (Wait for BUZZ response)
"Stand-by TK28 with 'Homeless' inject". (Wait for BUZZ)

It is important to wait for the buzz each time, otherwise you might stand-by two machines, and then hear two buzzes. Now is that a 'yes' from two machines or a 'no' from one?

## Run cues

When you run a VT or TK machine, again try to give the machine number at the same time as the run command. This, of course, isn't necessary if you only have one play-in machine, but it does help enormously, if you have a hectic and noisy gallery, with three or four play-in machines.

Start an insert watch when you run the machine as a back up to the ident clock or TK leader, but do look up to check they have run correctly and that your count is in sync with the real insert countdown.

On occasions you may have to work to a late 'in' cue, in order to lose the start of a clip, perhaps for timing reasons.  In this instance VT will spin back ten seconds from the 'in'.

You won't then have any kind of visual backup to your count and will have to trust the insert watch. DO REMEMBER TO FLICK BACK THE WATCH AT ZERO FOR THE INSERT TIMING.

## Countdowns

Counting in and out of inserts is vital for the smooth running of a programme. It is important to keep your count rhythmical, so that the information you provide for the gallery is clear and easy on the ear. For example, if you have to rehearse a short segment which involves running one or more inserts in, perhaps in trail making, pick a clear segment off the main studio clock and count in ten seconds from that, running your first insert at the required point, either at five or three seconds.

The studio clock helps to maintain your rhythm, and also gives you a guide when the insert clock has gone to black.

It is worth practising a smooth count : "Ten, nine, eight, seven, six — run VT — four, three, two, one, zero. It is very important to remember the word zero, because it gives everyone the point at which either to speak, fade up, mix or cue, and for you to start your watch ... so whatever you are counting to, precede the count with an ident.

Anticipate your count by a couple of seconds to give you time to say

"Counting into the programme..."
"Counting out of VT....."
"Counting to Aston super..."
"Counting to up sound ..."
"Counting out of VT..."
"Counting to pre-fade..."
"Counting to the end of the programme..."

Let us use the example of a clip of VT, of 3'50".

Once on to the clip, announce how long it is. "Three minutes fifty on VT, (and then repeat the time) three minutes fifty".

| At 50" | — 3 minutes left on VT, three minutes |
|--------|----------------------------------------|
| At 1'50" | — 2 minutes left on VT, two minutes |
| At 2'50" | — 1 minute left on VT, one minute |
| At 3'20" | — 30 seconds left on VT, thirty seconds, the out words/cue is: (give details) |
| At 3'30" | — 20 seconds left on VT, twenty seconds |
| At 3'40" | — counting out of VT: ten, nine, eight...etc. |

To achieve a smooth count on, say, the final count out of this insert, start by speaking at 3'38" — so your ten-second count is smooth and easy to listen to. Remember you are not just counting for your entertainment, the presenter could well be subbing a link to meet your count, and needs a smooth rhythm to make things easier.

Some directors and programme styles prefer a fifteen-second pointer, rather than the twenty-second one to give their information prior to your final count out. Adapt to their preferences but, by making the timings as above, it makes checking at a glance that much easier, especially in a fast-moving news programme.

Don't forget to watch the monitors as you are counting out of an insert. The director may choose to come out of it early, for timing or artistic reasons. If he does, don't keep counting to your heart's content to the end of the given duration, just stop, if possible noting down the transmitted duration (for your post-production paperwork) — the original duration now means nothing. New PAs will tend to write timing information on the script prior to recording/transmission. The more experienced PA will be able to read her watch without writing anything down.

## Counting in and out of the programme

Once you know your 'on-air' time from presentation, watch the clock and give everyone regular countdowns into the programme. During a hectic rehearsal period up to transmission, it is essential that you keep track. If at base, you will tend to get two-minute flashing lights from presentation, followed by a cue dot sequence. Count in loud and clear. (See Chapter 11, *The Lightning Guide to Live Galleries*, for details).

## VT logging

Make an accurate log of what actually happens during the recording. Give shot number, duration, reasons for re-takes, etc.

## Time code

The easiest way to log your recording is using time code, which can either be 'real time' or 'tape time'. It will be at least a six-figure number, and could be more if frames are included in the number. For example, 15:34:26:18 = three thirty-four, twenty-six seconds and eighteen frames.

## Note taking

Don't take notes in shorthand. Find a way of writing without looking, if you need to keep your eyes on the monitors. Write in some abbreviated way, so that the director can read your notes immediately — there won't be time to transcribe them.

Don't give messages to artists yourself, unless specifically requested to do so by the director.

### VT spool numbers

Make sure you don't leave the gallery without noting the spool numbers after your studio; in a large organisation they can disappear forever with your precious recording, never to be seen again! This is especially important if you are recording an OB off site or using a facilities house. The tapes may be needed urgently for an editing session. A lot of time can be wasted tracking down the engineer who recorded them in the hope that he remembers.

### Script checks

In a live current affairs or news studio it is vital that there is a script check before going on air, so everyone is working on the same programme order. Make sure your script is in the correct order.

### Shot calling

One of the PA's most important tasks in a gallery is to keep the place in the script for herself and everyone else. Current affairs scripts tend not to have shots, but each new story is numbered and on a separate page, so when the running order changes you can shuffle your scripts accordingly.

A rehearsed programme either live or recorded will often have shot numbers. As rehearsals progress new shots can be added or shots dropped, so it is important that the PA keeps up to date with all the changes and announces them clearly as they happen.

The cameramen will be relying on the PA calling shots to know where they are on their cards. During meal breaks, it helps enormously if the PA goes on to the studio floor and checks through the camera cards to make sure all the changes are included.

You need to call shots loud and clear in the gallery, giving all relevant information; there is no point in muttering to yourself as no one will be able to hear you.

Different types of script layout are illustrated in Chapter 12 but, whatever the layout, the job of shot calling will remain the same.

If there is a really fast section, you may not have time to call both the shot number and the next camera: in which case call the numbers only, so everyone knows where they are and the vision mixer will remember which camera is next. If you have added lots of extra shots and you are into the high numbers with a drama production, let us say: shots 124, 124A, 124B, 124C, 124D, 124E, etc. with the agreement of the cameraman, director and vision mixer, you could get away with just saying A, B, C, D, E.

In those really fast sequences, if you can hold your script up away from the surface of the gallery desk, your eye will have less distance to travel between the script and the monitors and you will be able to read faster.

When starting to shot call at the very beginning of a script, precede the shot number with the word 'shot' until you have passed the number of cameras you have on the studio floor. Otherwise things can get rather complicated. For example:

> One, three next.
> Two, one next.
> Three, two next.
> Four, one next.

So assuming you have three cameras it would be far less confusing to say:

> Shot one, three next.
> Shot two, one next.
> Shot three, two next.
> Four, one next.

Some beginners to shot calling put one finger on the shot number and another on the next camera, and then run their fingers down the page, in order not to lose sight of their place. Others mark their scripts with a light pencil mark, circling the shot number and running a line down to the next camera, so that they do not get tongue tied in a fast sequence. It could also prove useful in a sequence where two people are talking, and the dialogue in each case is rather short.

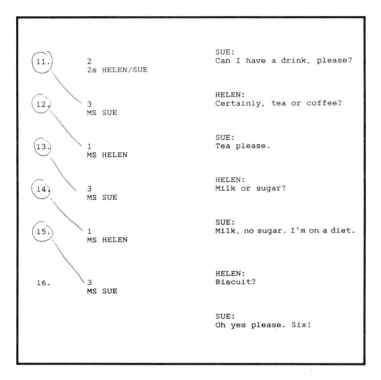

```
11.      2              SUE:
         2s HELEN/SUE   Can I have a drink, please?


12.      3              HELEN:
         MS SUE         Certainly, tea or coffee?


13.      1              SUE:
         MS HELEN       Tea please.


14.      3              HELEN:
         MS SUE         Milk or sugar?


15.      1              SUE:
         MS HELEN       Milk, no sugar. I'm on a diet.


16.      3              HELEN:
         MS SUE         Biscuit?


                        SUE:
                        Oh yes please. Six!
```

### Honesty is the best policy

Last, but by no means least, if you have made a mistake along the line with anything connected with the studio which can be rectified, do own up to it. Admitting your mistakes is always a hard thing to do, but far better than jeopardising the programme. If you are new to studios, ask for help and support. If you know something should be re-recorded for any reason, tell someone.

If your timings are wrong, let the producer know as soon as possible. If you are lost with shot calling, keep quiet until you can pick up again; the vision mixer will usually step into the breach.

# Chapter 10

# Timings & Time Charts

Where would a PA be without a stopwatch? Whether on location or in the studio a PA always has at least one stopwatch, either slung round her neck or glued to her hand.

I will start this chapter by dealing with ways of coping with your stopwatch, showing you a few tricks which will help with timing where maths is not involved! I will then move to ways of keeping track of the timing of a programme's with the help of the time chart.

## Let your watch do the work...

The art of using a stopwatch is to let it do most of the hard work when it comes to maths. You've got to be able to interpret what you see and use it, without mindlessly reeling off figures which you don't understand. Part of the problem with a programme with a fixed duration is the fear of getting your maths wrong and not completing the programme on time.

## Watch blindness

Many PAs talk of 'watch blindness', when they are involved in a hectic, timed programme and everyone in the gallery wants to know the state of play as far as time is concerned. The simple solution is to minimise the requirement for maths at all. Providing you use an ordinary watch face for your insert and never a digital watch, you can save yourself a lot of calculation.

## Digital watches

These are best used for overall timings. Most will count forwards or backwards and some can be pre-set to pick up during a stop/start recording to keep up with an overall timing. Some will also add up in minutes and seconds to calculate an overall timing.

## Pieces of cake

If you look at the face of a standard stop watch, you can see it is divided up into slices, rather like a cake, into quarters then into 5-second segments.

Use the watch face to do your timings for you. You don't have to know precisely what 30 seconds back from 2'49" is — you can read the face of your watch and see where thirty seconds should be, if necessary using a pencil or pen to lie across the face of the watch.

## Insert timings

If you are calculating back timings out of a sequence in a programme of say 5'49" in duration, look at the watch. Whole minutes left on your item duration, i.e. 4 minutes left will be at 1'49" on your watch, 3 minutes left will be at 2'49" and so on.

When you get to within the last minute, look at the watch face, it will do your maths for you. If 5'49" is one small blip away from a big blip on the watch face, then 30" back will be directly opposite at one blip before a big black blip, at 5'19"; 20" back is therefore at 5'29", and your 10" count out will start at 5'39".

I always find it easier to work out timings in 10" chunks, i.e. 30", 20" and 10" cues, as then they all end with a nine. However, some people and places prefer a 15" check rather than the 20", in which case you've got to lose the convenience of having the same number at the end of each cue.

As a double check, in this case, when you are counting out as you say the word "nine" of the count-out, the watch will read

5'40", so what you *say* and what you *see* add up to the total duration, and you know you are on track.

If you can get to grips with reading the watch face instead of doing maths, the fear of working on a fast-moving, timed programme soon disappears.

### You are in charge of programme timings

Remember, you are likely to be the only person in the gallery with a stopwatch. So when your over-excitable producer wants to know instantly how the programme is doing for time, (always at the most inconvenient moment) and if you are the sort who needs a few unharassed moments to work out your timings, stall for time and tell him anything! He'll go away happy with his new-found knowledge, giving you a few moments to work things out accurately and then announce precisely where you are.

It's not as crazy as it sounds. After all, you can't be that far adrift. If you were on a 5-minute insert, and only a few seconds ago you announced 3 minutes left on VT — say "just under 3 minutes left on VT". Then do your sums and announce the exact time. A time chart, too, will give you an overall picture of the programme timings and I shall go into that in more detail later.

So a little bluff can go a long way, but it can become a dangerous habit to get into if you don't really know what you are doing. When you are new to timed programmes and unsure of yourself in the gallery, a little bluff to convince everyone else that you are absolutely in control will give you the breathing space needed to get to grips with your timings.

### How many watches

Normally, you would use an overall watch and an insert watch. If you have too many watches you may become confused about which one is timing which piece of your programme. Some PAs choose to add another watch for an opt within the main programme.

Do make sure there is no chance of confusing your watches. If you need an overall watch, use the desk-mounted watch and put the lock on to prevent you flicking it back in a moment of relapse during the programme.

Never let your insert watch out of your hand. If you are right-handed, have a pen or pencil in your right hand and your insert watch in your left, or *vice versa*.

If you need to start a third for an opt, then have another in a clearly marked place on the desk, perhaps with a sticky label next to it. If you can organise yourself, so that watches always stay in the same place on the desk you shouldn't get confused.

**Have confidence in your watch and the gallery will have confidence in you**

In every situation nerves are infectious and once the rest of the gallery have lost confidence in you, they will be on your back all the more to check up on how you are doing — which doesn't help anybody.

So it can be a losing battle unless you convince everyone quickly that you know exactly what you are doing. The more you can do to familiarise yourself with the contents of a programme before you get into the gallery, the happier you will feel about it.

**Oops! My watch has stopped**

The PA's nightmare in the gallery is to look down at the insert watch and find that it has stopped. Don't panic. What other points of reference do you have? Try and learn to note the 'in' time of your programme off the main studio clock. Then work your timing from that. Many gallery PAs choose to do that anyway. You can frequently be working to an off-air time rather than a programme duration. (See *Back and forward timings* p.83).

If all else fails, warn the gallery that your timings and counts will be wild. The editor or producer of the item may be in the gallery and can guide everyone through. Listen for the 'out' words and keep your fingers crossed.

## Last minute watches

The final minutes of a live current affairs or sports programme can be very hectic and some PAs start extra watches towards the end of the programme to guide them through the closing.

Some choose as far ahead as 10 minutes to the off-air time or to a fixed point at the end of the programme, (for example, the closing VT and credits). The point at which you start this extra watch is up to you, either 10 or 5 minutes to a fixed final point. This extra watch is particularly useful if the closing is very hectic, and you will be running several other inserts, or if presentation have given you an extremely awkward off-air time — let us say 17.19.42.

BBC Sports department have come up with a lovely phrase — "counting to stopping talking", which means the PA's count will be to the time the presenter stops talking and the closing VT and credits appear. In this example, assuming the closing insert and credits ran for 30 seconds, the 'stopping talking' time is 17.19.12.

You start your 10 minute watch at 17.09.12, and count out through the complicated closing using this watch, which has simply shifted the awkward segment of 12" to the top of the watch. It is far easier to say "9 minutes to stopping talking" when your 10 minute watch says 1 minute, than working back to 17.10.12 on the studio clock. It sounds complicated, but believe me it makes a hectic closing much simpler.

## What was all that about!

Many PAs will come out of a busy live magazine programme and have no idea what was in the programme. Everyone else will be talking about an interesting item, whilst you had your head buried in your watch and your time chart right the way through. Unless there are major changes, you should gradually be able to run the gallery and enjoy the programme!!

# TIME CHARTS

Time charts are the easiest, and most reliable way of keeping track of timings during a programme.

If the programme is to be recorded and edited later you will need to take editing notes of takes and re-takes, but you will also need to know how long your pre-recorded programme is in order to edit it to the correct duration.

Alternatively, you may try to record the programme 'as live' and want to record the items to as near the correct duration as possible.

Basically the elements you need for a time chart fall into a fairly standard format, which can be modified for specific programme needs.

It is far better for the purposes of your time chart, to break up the programme into smaller sections, whilst keeping linked items together. The following pattern of columns has emerged as a standard way of dividing the programme information:

• A column to identify the item  and the ingredients of that item.

• A column with the individual timings of the elements within that item.

• A column totalling the ingredients within that item.

• A column to estimate the running time so far for the programme.

• A column for actual timings as you record or transmit your programme.

As you record or transmit the programme, complete the last column as you go along, and that's done all the sums for you.

The following example of a time chart illustrates these points.

| ITEM | | INDIV TIME | ITEM TIME | RUNNING TIME | OVERALL TIMING |
|---|---|---|---|---|---|
| 1. | | | | | |
| Opening | VT | 0'30" | | | |
| Sequence | link | 0'20" | | | |
| | VT | 1'26" | 2'16" | 2'16" | |
| 2. | | | | | |
| House | link | 1'20" | | | |
| | VT | 2'00" | | | |
| | INT | 3'30" | 6'50" | 9'06 | |

## Rounding up and rounding down

Having given the above illustration, I would now modify that still further, to make life even easier.

Rather than having 2'16" as the item time for the first item, I would call it 2'15". You haven't lost a second, but it simplifies matters if the running order changes during the programme and you have to move an item up or down the running order. Far better to know that you had 2'15" to place further down the programme, than 2'16". Similarly, I would call the 9'06", 9'05".

It is a fact that directors and producers always seem to have an uncanny knack of asking how the programme is doing for time at the most awkward point, so rounding up and rounding down your totals makes it far easier when glancing across at an overall watch.

Before going to the gallery, fill in as much of your time chart as you can. The producer will have mapped out ideal times for all the items within the programme, so at least you know the estimated time for each segment even if none of the insert items are edited or the scripted links finalised.

Once you get the scripts, time them. The normal rate of speech is three words a second — use this as a starting point, until you know your presenter better and make any necessary adjustments.

Allow more time for long complicated words, foreign place names and dignitaries. Descriptions of things and lists of statistics always take longer, especially if they are accompanied by a graphics sequence with animations, so allow for pauses. Also, check the content of the script, for example, it may be very light-hearted and need to be more drawn out than usual. I have already mentioned that dates can catch you out, so do read them aloud as you time a link.

Having worked through the timings for your programme, you will have a number of gaps left for the interviews, discussions, or demonstrations. These are the live programme PA's lifeline.

The following running order with flexible items will give you an idea of how to work out a time chart for a thirty-minute programme:

| | |
|---|---|
| VT. opening titles | 0.30" |
| opening link | 0.20" |
| VT sequence 2 (traffic) | 1.26" |
| | |
| link | 1.20" |
| VT seq 3 (house building) | 2.00" |
| discussion | T.B.A. |
| | |
| link | 0.15" |
| VT seq 4 (dogs) | 0.45" |
| demonstration | T.B.A. |
| | |
| link | 0.25" |
| interview (inc. VT seq 4 - 20") | T.B.A. |
| link | 0.15" |
| music item | 2.15" |
| back ref outro | 0.20" |
| | |
| trail tomorrow's prog | 0.20" |
| weather | 0.30" |
| link | 0.15" |
| VT seq 5 (daffodils) | 1.04" |
| | |
| TOTAL DURATION | 30.00 |

## Buffers

Flexible items, buffers — call them what you will — are the elastic in the programme which allow a perfect fit into the transmission time slot. In the following example, the programme duration is 30 minutes; if you add up all the known timings you get 12 minutes, leaving 18 minutes to allocate to the 'T.B.A.' items, the interview, the discussion and the demonstration.

The producer will then decide how best to divide up the available time and then you have a time chart to fit the programme duration. Obviously, it is in everyone's best interests to finalise timings before going into the gallery.

Ideally, try to run each item as planned — for example, the demonstration should run 5'30". However, if the first interview overran by 30 seconds, bringing you out of that item at 16'05" instead of 15'35", you would need to tighten your timings somewhere. You would then move down to your next flexible item which would be the discussion, and you would have to run that to 8'30" to bring you out of that item on time at 25'00". Or if the producer preferred, you would keep the discussion to 9'00" and lose the 30 seconds out of your demonstration.

Once you know how much time is available to divide between the flexible items, work to those timings until an insert comes in to throw the calculations and then you will need to shorten here and there to accommodate new information.

It is important to remember that the editorial decisions are the responsibility of the producer, so if a major item has been dropped or your estimated timings are a long way over or under and major changes have to be made, the editor or producer would decide what to drop and what to change, but it is your job to keep everyone informed.

Your time chart should show precisely how far over or under you are at any given moment in the programme. You can then confidently make the necessary adjustments to keep yourself on track and bring the programme out on time.

| ITEM | | INDIV TIME | ITEM TIME | RUNNING TIME | OVERALL TIMING |
|---|---|---|---|---|---|
| 1. | | | | | |
| Opening | VT | 0'30" | | | |
| sequence | link | 0'20" | | | |
| | VT | 1'26" | 2'16" | 2'15" | |
| | | | | | |
| 2. | | | | | |
| House | link | 1'20" | | | |
| | VT | 2'00" | | | |
| | INT. | 3'30" | 6'50" | 9'05" | |
| | | | | | |
| 3. | | | | | |
| Dogs | link | 0'15" | | | |
| | VT | 0'45" | | | |
| | demo | 5'30" | 6'30" | 15'35" | |
| | | | | | |
| 4. | | | | | |
| Training | link | 0'25" | | | |
| (inc.VT) | disc. | 9'00" | 9'25" | 25'00" | |
| | | | | | |
| 5. | | | | | |
| Song | link | 0'15" | | | |
| | music | 2'35" | | | |
| | outro | 0'20" | 3'10" | 28'10" | |
| | | | | | |
| 6. | | | | | |
| Goodnight | trail | 0'20" | | | |
| | weather | 0'30" | | | |
| | link | 0'15" | | | |
| | VT | 0'45" | 1'50" | 30'00" | |

The joy of working with a time chart is that nearly all the work is done prior to the actual gallery. During the run up to the programme, you can work out how it will run. Providing you have filled in all the variables, even if they are only the producer's estimates of item duration, you can calculate where any likely 'hot spots' might occur within the programme.

## Pre-fades

Another simple way to bring the programme out on time is to have the closing item as a pre-fade. This is usually applicable when the programme ends with supered credits over live studio shots with taped music. It can be run in at the correct time to bring the programme out on time, but the viewer won't see or hear it until the director chooses.

Obviously, the neatest way to end the programme is for it to finish on the last note of music. But you may find the ideal length for the credits is 30 seconds and the music lasts 1'15". So work back 1'15" on your time chart, namely 28'45" and that is the point where the closing music is run as a pre-fade.

The final item of the programme is still running and the music is not faded up until the correct cue, namely 29'30" in order to run 30 seconds of credits with the last 30 seconds of music. Having pre-faded the music, the programme will now end neatly at the end of the music.

## Keeping everyone informed of changes

You are the only person in the gallery with the time chart and the stopwatches, so every time you can, let the producer and director know how you are doing for time, so they can decide what to do. If changes have to be made, their decisions can then be passed on immediately to all those who need to know such as the presenters.

If they have been planning a 5-minute interview and, due to other items in the programme over-running, the time has to be reduced, it is important that they know immediately, so that their questions can be adjusted accordingly.

## Boxed timings

There is usually a place in a script which is the last point of flexibility within the programme, if you are to come out on time. Put a large red box round this and, with luck, it will be at the end of a weather check or something easily shortened or dropped.

## Fixed points within your programme

Quite often in a magazine programme which has a regional element to it, you will need to opt the regions in and out at one or more points during the main programme. Mark your time chart clearly with these points and count to them, preferably from fifteen, to give the regions as much warning as possible.

This also applies to commercial breaks or any other fixed point in the programme. You may well, for example, have a region joining your programme midway and they will need a count to the 'in' point.

## Back and forward timings

Programmes will be timed in different ways. Some will work to an agreed on-air time and fixed duration. Others will work to an off-air time regardless of when they went on air. This will then mean rapid work on your time chart to work out back timings to the agreed off-air time. For example, if you are working on a regional opt, current affairs programme, which went on air three minutes late due to an overrun from the network news programme, you still have to work to an off-air time for the opt back into the network.

The first half of your time chart might look similar to the previous example, but at some stage towards the end of the programme you will need to have off-air times working backwards through the remaining items in the programme.

There may be a fixed time to hit your closing music or final VT, or perhaps it's just a case of the presenter filling with an unscripted *ad lib* weather forecast. Usually, given the point of no return on your time chart, you would work off the studio clock, counting out of the inserts/links/programme to the off-air time.

## Digital clock counters in the gallery

In news and current affairs programmes, it is often possible to have a digital counter in the gallery, which will count down during the programme from the total programme duration, giving you the remaining time on your programme. Towards the end of a hectic news programme this can prove invaluable.

Do beware, however, in case a previous programme's over-run affects your programme duration.

Like everything, the PA must be adaptable. Design your own ideal time chart if there isn't one that suits the style of the programme. Give yourself enough space for changes in the running order and don't make each section too small, as the studio lighting can be quite dark and you need to write clear, bold figures which can be read at a glance.

Using an A4 sheet, don't aim to have more than eight sequences per page, remembering that each sequence may have three or four elements. See how the programme falls into a set pattern and then decide on the best design. Things like double lines at key points in the programme may help to draw your eye to the on-coming awkward point in the programme.

Better to have two or three pages of a time chart, than the whole programme squeezed on to one page.

# Chapter 11

# The Lightning Guide to
# Live Galleries

The first and most important thing to remember about live galleries, is DON'T PANIC!! They are not as difficult as people think. The only difference is ... you don't get a second chance to do them again. Some PAs would not have it any other way.

There is, however, extra pressure for accurate timings, complete concentration, a cool head and nerves of steel. Once on-air it is up to you to bring the programme out on time.

## Preparation

Ring presentation as soon as you can on the day of transmission, to check up on your programme duration and rough on-air time. These can still change, but at least it's a guideline.

- Check the running order early in the day to assess any potential difficulties with the programme.

- Start your time chart as soon as you can during the day, filling in the gaps as you go along (see p.81 for layout).

- See as many inserts as you can.

- If you cannot view the insert clips, try to get details from the person who is editing the inserts. NEVER rely on anyone else's timings.

- Get any optional 'ins' and 'outs' of clips if you can, it will help if things start going wrong on air.

- If relevant to the insert, find out if there is a nice long shot at the end of the piece to allow a mix off the clip; if so, make sure it is marked on the script.

- As the scripted links come through — time them for yourself. Make allowances for long words and complicated names. Also allow for the date, etc. — 1991 looks like one short word, but it is of course three words. Descriptions and lists also take longer to say.

- Start to compile a name super list.

## Cue dots

This is the easiest and most efficient way for presentation to get a live programme on air. In the BBC, the cue dots appear in the top left-hand corner of the screen approximately thirty seconds before transmission; they go off exactly ten seconds before you go on air. The ITV networks put a graded square cue dot in the top right-hand corner approximately one minute before a junction or commercial break and take it off exactly five seconds before the junction.

## Pre-flight checks with presentation

In your pre-flight checks with presentation, you need to confirm all the necessary details to ensure a smooth junction. They need details of the start of your programme: does it begin in the usual way with opening titles or a tease? Are there any alterations to your regular programme pattern, such as the absence of a regular presenter who might unwittingly be mentioned in a presentation link?

Check your programme duration and give a clear outline of the end sequence. You may have a complicated closing sequence where your count might not prove too clear. Give as much detail as possible, such as credit duration, music duration, last credit — especially important if you have an unusual close, like a false ending. If they don't know, they could fade you off-air before the intended time. Confirm how you will count out of the programme, if possible with a fifteen-second final count to give presentation enough time to run a trail or another programme off the back of your count.

## Other warnings to presentation

Warn presentation if there are any unusual sequences in the programme. A sequence in black and white or a simulated picture breakdown could give the presentation engineer a heart attack if he isn't pre-warned. Also warn if the programme ends with an uncontrollable item, like the programme's pet doing something which won't necessarily stick to the script or the agreed duration.

### Noting on-air time: a useful back up

If you can, make a note of your on-air time as you hit transmission, off the studio clock. The technical co-ordinator will check it is in sync with presentation.

If your live programme is away from base, do make sure the engineering manager has checked the scanner clock with the speaking clock and presentation, as they are notoriously unreliable. Then, if your overall watch fails, you would have a second back-up timing from the main clock. It means extra maths, but at least you have a chance. (Always take a spare watch with you when away from base).

Presentation also makes a note of your on-air time, so if all else fails you could ring them and find out when you are expected off air.

### Don't let your watch out of your hand

Keep your insert watch in your hand (your left hand if you are right handed and *vice versa*), so that you won't lose it or confuse it with another watch.

### Interim timings

Another useful guide is to jot timings down at each paragraph during rehearsals, so that when cuts are made, you can work out how much time you have saved. If you have more than one rehearsal, colour code your timings, so you should then have a good idea if the presenters are spreading on transmission. However, people usually speed up, if anything, once the red light is on.

### Giving timings to your presenters

When giving timings to presenters or a floor/stage manager, always repeat the timings — "two minutes left on interview, two minutes". Presenters like timings in nice round fifteen-second chunks. They never want to hear "three minutes, forty two seconds left on this VTR".

Quite often if a presenter is concentrating on an interview, he will only pick up your voice as you are saying "... left on interview..." so that's why you should repeat the time.

### Be prepared for the worst

There is no escaping the fact, that whilst it might not show on the television at home, things do go wrong with live pro- grammes. Keep your eyes and ears open all the time. Be a real pessimist, think of all the things that could go wrong with the programme, have a solution up your sleeve and if they don't happen — well you've survived another smooth show.

### A little time up your sleeve for emergencies

If you have new presenters, or a very chatty interviewee, lie a little about your timings and bring them out a whisker early, just in case you have a complicated VT closing which you have to hit on the nail — a few seconds in hand make all the difference and can save the day.

Don't get flustered by directors and producers wanting to know how the programme is doing for time. The time chart is yours. Fob them off with an answer — after all you can't be that far out — and then do your sums and announce the exact time. Often those few unhassled moments help. If you have worked out an accurate time chart to start with, you really can never be that far adrift. Just look at your overall watch and work out from your time chart where you are. It really is very simple.

The secret is to bluff with confidence. Make sure everyone thinks you are on top of things. The moment they suspect nerves they will want reassurance and will constantly ask you for information and timings, just when you need some thinking time.

### Getting off-air smoothly

As you approach the end, tell presentation if your running time is OVER or UNDER. It helps them if you can keep a running commentary on how you are doing for time:

"Three minutes left to the end of the programme, two minutes left on this interview, one minute to closing music and credits. Pres. — we're about ten seconds over at this stage."

### Getting on-air when away from base: a few extra problems

Make sure you can see a feed of network (or wherever your presentation department is) for cue dots. If there is any doubt, because you are out of London, the engineering manager can arrange a special feed for you to get on air. If that fails, you may have a direct 'phone link to presentation or you may need to rely on a standard BT telephone line.

Check with the network director before going on air, that you can see the dots — you must always ensure that you have enough time to go through proper checks and confirm your duration and estimated on-air time with presentation. Find out what programme precedes yours in case it overruns and causes problems, e.g. tennis or cricket.

Make sure presentation know how the programme starts, so that they can introduce it correctly. You should have sent them a couple of scripts in advance, but this is not always possible.

Clearly outline how your programme should end: give the duration of credits and closing music, PA count out, etc; if there is a potential problem at the end, ask them to listen in on programme talkback (if they have it) so you can shout any alterations in the panic of the last moments rather than ringing them up.

Obviously a lot of OB events are unpredictable towards the end and, if you are working on one you may need to talk presentation through the closing and tell them when they can take the programme off air.

Above all remember — it is not open heart surgery and you are not flying Concorde ... it's only television!

Oh, P.S. ... enjoy it!

# Chapter 12

# The Camera Script
# & Camera Cards

A camera script is essential for the smooth running of a programme. It contains all the necessary information to put the programme on air the way the director intended.

### The layout of the script

The layout of a script can vary slightly, but a standard format has evolved over the years, so that whatever the programme, the technical operations crew, vision mixer, floor manager and everyone else will not have to waste time trying to understand a new script format.

Directly or indirectly, it will be used by practically everyone working on the show, but because of the amount of information involved, each individual has got to mark up the original script so that his or her responsibilities stand out clearly.

It is important that if changes have happened following printing and prior to distribution, corrections are made to essential production copies, namely those for the director, vision mixer, floor manager, technical co-ordinator, lighting director and sound supervisor. Where necessary you would also have to make all the changes to the camera cards for the crew.

Divide the script page by an imaginary line down the centre of the page; use the left-hand side of the camera script for the shot numbers, camera numbers and positions and moves, the cut line or details of transitions between shots and a brief description of the shot.

The main body of the dialogue and action is found just to the right of the invisible line down the centre of the script and to the far right is all the sound information, such as booms, grams/tape and sound effects, etc.

It is therefore important to place information associated with sound on the right-hand side and information associated with vision on the left, so that the vision and sound crews can quickly mark up their scripts, knowing that all the information they need to know is in the usual place. This is particularly important on a fast-moving, live programme.

### Recording breaks

These should be clearly marked across the span of the script page, giving details of things such as costume changes or flattage to be moved within the break.

### Boxed information

Camera moves or lighting instructions which need to be known by everyone can be placed in boxes on the appropriate side of the script.

Don't be selfish and type information which you need on the script, when that space could be used for information for some-one else. Use your preparatory time to add the information you require on your script only, such as stand-by cues and run cues.

### Outside sources/insert material

Mark outside sources clearly with a line right across the script to differentiate them from any other sources in the studio. Give all necessary/known information such as 'ins' and 'outs'.

### Top and bottom of pages

When you get to the last shot on a fully shot-numbered script, write the next camera number at the bottom of the script, in the left hand-corner. Then at the top of the next page, put the shot number you are on, plus the camera number for the next shot in the top left-hand corner. That way no one forgets what has just happened, nor are they taken by surprise by the next shot near the top of the following page.

You should, in any case, always split your script, so that you can see what is coming up next. But you must never split a sentence.

As there is limited space to write camera instructions on a camera script, a shorthand of standard terms has developed and is universally accepted by both production teams and technical crews alike. A list of these can be found on p.98.

### Numbering pages

You may well be recording your script out of sequence, so it is important to re-number your pages in recording order, usually written in after the camera script has been typed. But do be careful not to lose sight of the story order page numbers.

### As-directed sequences

In some programmes, parts may be fully scripted while others are 'as directed'. When there are as-directed sequences, ample space needs to be left on the scripts and camera cards (if used) so that shots and notes can be inserted.

### Spacing

Never try to save money by saving on a script. It is truly a false economy. Remember that your typing of the script is only the start and many others have got to add information to it, so leave them space.

### Shot sizes

To speed things along in rehearsal, certain shot sizes have become standardized and rather than a director edging a cameraman in and out to find the right framing, (the 'golden shot' method of direction!), he can quote a recognised shot size and the cameraman and boom operator will know precisely what he means.

### News and current affairs layout

In news and current affairs, the programme script will not be a continuous document with shot numbers and camera numbers, but will consist of separate, numbered sequences for each story. This allows the running order to change, but keeps all the elements associated with each segment together.

During the run up to transmission the director will allocate cameras and, with the vision mixer and sound crew, mark up scripts accordingly.

In many current affairs programmes, the most important document is the **running order**. A complete running order is really a shorthand version of the programme's script, listing sequences and the elements involved within each item.

In current affairs programmes, the camera crew will generally use the running order, instead of camera cards, allowing greater flexibility during the live transmission.

### The computer revolution

There is a great danger that the nightmare of typing a mammoth script late into the night, altering shots which the director promised not to include, may be a thing of the past! There has been a recent revolution in the use of computers for script typing, which should prove to be a great relief to all PAs.

There are a variety of established computer systems already used by news and current affairs programmes, where the journalists or producers type the text directly into the machine, formatting as they go.

Additionally, certain systems add up all the durations of the scripted links and inserts and at the press of a button provide you with an accurately-timed running order. If an item is dropped or changed, the information is fed into the computer and the running order is updated accordingly.

There are also now various computer programmes which help other types of script layout. They will separate the left and right side of the script and let you work independently on either. The more sophisticated ones insert your cut lines as you type in the shots and even accommodate the insertion of a late shot, by knocking on the shot numbers accordingly right the way through the script. Some even have a facility to do camera cards, where you press the button and the computer divides up all your camera shots and lays them out on the appropriate cards.

On pp.101-112 there are some examples of different script layouts taken from a cross section of BBC programmes. As mentioned, the formats follow the set style although adaptations are made to suit specialist needs — not always with the total agreement of everyone working on the programme!

### Hold the front page ...

Another important aspect of the camera script is the front page. To save yourself time on a long-running regular programme devise a master template for the front page. It is worth getting this out of the way as soon as possible, filling in the gaps as you get the relevant information.

There is bound to be an old script of a previous programme similar to yours which you can use. It should contain all the necessary information for those contributing to your programme such as:

- The programme title
- The episode number
- The costing number (with relevant insert numbers)
- The transmission date (if known)
- The recording date
- The studio details (place of recording)
- A brief outline of recording schedule
- Editing dates and times
- Names of production team
- Names of technical and craft crew
- Names of guests and contributors
- A list of useful telephone numbers.

### Useful Information

The next page of your script should contain any extra information which will help the recording day run smoothly, such as reminders about arrival times and parking arrangements for guests.

Bear in mind that special requirements may have to be made for guests with animals or valuable props. This service will be especially helpful for a floor manager who may well only be with your programme for the day.

### Recording schedule

As you draw closer to your recording day, the director/floor manager/production manager will work out a recording schedule, containing all recording breaks, costume changes, etc. It may highlight a problem they otherwise would not have discovered, such as impossible make-up and costume changes or awkward camera moves. Some PAs use this schedule to mark down editing notes, keeping it to one side for an at-a-glance way of checking up on what has been recorded and what still needs to be done.

### Floorplans

Early in the production planning stage, following meetings with the producer and director, the designer will draw the sets on to a floor plan. This is a scale drawing of the studio floor, divided up into numbered squares, so that any point on the plan can be pin-pointed by two reference numbers, just like reading a map. There are corresponding numbers around the studio walls so that the precise point marked on the floor plan can be found on the studio floor. This reference system is used by everyone — designer, scene crew, cameraman, floor manager, lighting director and programme director.

Also marked on the floor plan are the positions of all the lighting barrels, scenery hoists, camera cabling points and microphone points, water, gas, electricity outlets and, of course, the doors. This is important from the point of view of safety.

It is essential that everyone works to the same plan, so that after the planning meeting and designs have been drawn on the plan, lighting, sound and the director can work on their specific tasks to bring the production into the studio.

The AFM will mark out a copy of the plan on the rehearsal room floor, so that the artists have an exact outline of the sets to rehearse with; the scene crew, when rigging the studio, will know precisely where each piece of set is to be placed and the camera crew can cable up as required from the information shown.

# SCRIPT TERMS

| | |
|---|---|
| A/B | before /as above |
| BCU | Big close shot |
| B/E | Black edge |
| B/G | Background |
| B/P | Back projection |
| C | Centre |
| Cam L | Camera left |
| Cam R | Camera right |
| CAP | Caption |
| COF | Centre of frame |
| CPU | Caption projection unit |
| CU/CS | Close up/Close shot |
| CSO | Colour separation overlay |
| C2S | Close 2-shot |
| DFS/DV | Digital frame store/digital video effects (e.g. Quantel, E-flex, A.D.O., N.E.C.) |
| d.s. | Downstage |
| fav | Favouring |
| F/D | Fade down |
| f/g | Foreground |
| F/O | fade out |
| F/P | Front projection fr. |
| fr L (R) | Frame left (right) |
| F/U | Fade up |
| fwd. | Forward |
| FX | Effects |
| Grams. | Music or sound FX from gramophone records |
| HA | High angle |
| L | Left |
| LA | Low angle |
| LS | Long shot |

| | |
|---|---|
| MCU/MCS | Medium close up/Medium close shot |
| Mic. | Microphone |
| MLS | Medium long shot |
| MS | Mid shot |
| M2S | Mid 2-shot |
| O/L | Overlay |
| OOF | Out of Frame |
| OOV | Out of vision |
| O/S | Over shoulder |
| Q | Cue |
| R | Right |
| Rec. | Recording |
| S. & V. | Sound and Vision |
| S/B | Standby |
| S/I | Superimpose |
| SOF | Sound on Film |
| SOT | Sound on 1/4" tape |
| SOVT | Sound on videotape |
| Spot FX | Sound effects physically made in the studio; not on disc or tape |
| TJ | Telejector slide |
| TK | Telecine |
| T/O | Take out |
| TX/tx | Transmission |
| u.s. | Upstage |
| VLS | Very long shot |
| VO | Voice over |
| VT | Videotape |
| WA | Wide angle |
| Xs | Across or crosses |
| 2s | 2-shot |

# OTHER TERMS

| Cameras | Vision Mixer | Others |
|---|---|---|
| Pan R or L | WIPE | FADE |
| JIB R or L | IRIS | TAPE |
| CRAB R or L | MIX | MUTE |
| CRANE up or down | CUT | |
| ELEVATE and DEPRESS | | |
| TRACK in and out | | |
| ZOOM in and out | | |
| FOCUS UP and DEFOCUS | | |
| TILT UP and DOWN | | |

## SCRIPT EXAMPLES

1.  SCRIPTED MAGAZINE PROGRAMME WITH
    SHOT NUMBERS  (p.101)
A good example, nice and clear and well laid out.
Includes shot numbers as it is a rehearsed programme.

2.  SCRIPTED MAGAZINE PROGRAMME
    WITHOUT SHOT NUMBERS  (p.102)
The text could be broken up more for easier reading.
VT insert information is typed in, but shots are worked
out during rehearsals and then written on the script.
No shot numbers are used.

3.  CURRENT AFFAIRS SCRIPT   (p.103)
No shot numbers as each item is given a sequence
number and a title to allow for running order flexibility
within a live current affairs programme.

4.  SPORTS PROGRAMME  (p.104)
Not a good example, although the department have
been using this layout for years, and say no one
ever complains (!) The cut lines have been put in front
of cues rather than at the end of the previous text,
meaning the vision mixers have to waste time drawing
in cut lines where they want them. The small type face
will cause problems in poor gallery lighting. Also far
too much on one page, not allowing space for notes.

5.  POP MUSIC SCRIPT LAYOUT (p.105)
Good clear layout for lyrics and music, showing split
bars and beats across shots. This programme also
includes details of composer and publisher required
for PasC.

6. CONVENTIONAL DRAMA SCRIPT (p.106)
Good clear layout. Blocking the dialogue helps for easy reading.

7. SITUATION COMEDY, NON-STANDARD (p.107)
Layout designed by an L.E. Director as he felt this was more logical, to have everything relating to a shot below the cut line. PAs and vision mixers tend to disagree.

8. UNSCRIPTED MAGAZINE PROGRAMME (p.108)
Still resembling a running order, with little dialogue, just pointers within a sequence.

9. SCRIPTED MAGAZINE (p.109)
Example of multi-pass CSO (or chromakey) script. Always laid out with a lot of space for vision mixer's notes.

10. MULTI-VOCAL OPERA (p.110)
Example of scripted format for an opera. Designed like this because the director for this studio recording could not read a music score. Also shows layout for ensemble voices.

11. MAGAZINE PROGRAMME RUNNING
        ORDER (p.111)
This includes item durations and cumulative timings. Used by the cameraman instead of camera cards and by those members of the production team, who only need the sequence order, not the dialogue.

12. CURRENT AFFAIRS RUNNING ORDER (p.112)
Used by cameramen instead of camera cards

# Specimen: Scripted Magazine Prog. with Shot Numbers

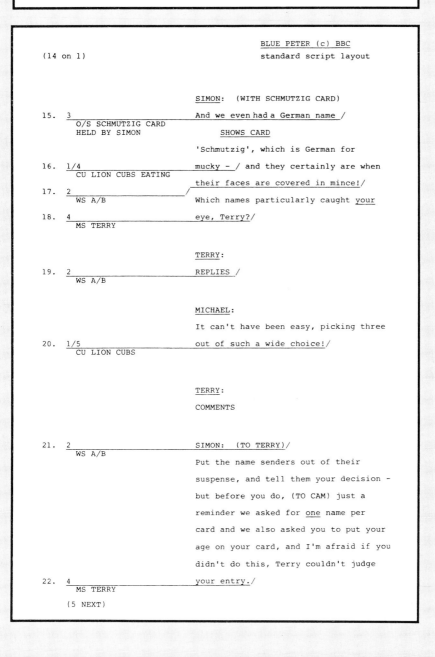

```
                                        BLUE PETER (c) BBC
        (14 on 1)                       standard script layout


                                        SIMON:  (WITH SCHMUTZIG CARD)
        15.  3                          And we even had a German name /
             O/S SCHMUTZIG CARD
             HELD BY SIMON              SHOWS CARD

                                        'Schmutzig', which is German for
        16.  1/4                        mucky - / and they certainly are when
             CU LION CUBS EATING
                                        their faces are covered in mince!/
        17.  2                     /
             WS A/B                      Which names particularly caught your

        18.  4                          eye, Terry?/
             MS TERRY


                                        TERRY:
        19.  2                          REPLIES /
             WS A/B

                                        MICHAEL:

                                        It can't have been easy, picking three
        20.  1/5                        out of such a wide choice!/
             CU LION CUBS


                                        TERRY:

                                        COMMENTS


        21.  2                          SIMON:  (TO TERRY)/
             WS A/B                      Put the name senders out of their

                                        suspense, and tell them your decision -

                                        but before you do, (TO CAM) just a

                                        reminder we asked for one name per

                                        card and we also asked you to put your

                                        age on your card, and I'm afraid if you

                                        didn't do this, Terry couldn't judge
        22.  4                          your entry./
             MS TERRY
             (5 NEXT)
```

# Specimen: Scripted Magazine Prog. without Shot Numbers

TRANSPORT OUTRO/PROMETHEUS/COMMS INTRO/VT

2 CU HOWARD **HOWARD i/v**

TOMORROW'S WORLD
(c) BBC

/STANDBY VT-12/

WIDEN TO SEE CAR

But the key to improving traffic flow

will be a revolution in communications.

1 CU CAR

SUPER SLIDE FILE WAVES

If every car/transmits its position to a

central computer, traffic can be routed

ANIMATE

efficiently just/like air traffic control.

ANIMATE

And if every car tells its neighbours

where it is/automatic systems could

2 WS

allow much close/ spacing between

TIGHTEN TO
HOWARD
CU

vehicles, tripling motorway capacity.

Sophisticated communications are going

to effect businesses and the home too.

/RUN VT-12/

So now we've a report from a country

that plans to play a major role in that

MIX

revolution, Singapore.

VT-12 (Dur: 2'58")

In: MUSIC

**COMMUNICATIONS**

S/I @     Angelina Fernandez

"Imagine this is......

Singapore Broadcasting Corp

S/I @     Daniel Wee

Out:  ... at twenty eight degrees

centigrade as  you wish."

Dur: 2'58"

-18-

# Specimen: Current Affairs

```
                                    NEWSROOM SOUTH EAST
                                    (c) BBC
                                    current affairs programme


            date      time    pdr id           dur: seq:pge

LONDON+   27 JUN 90     sb3   BATHS

----------------------------------------------------------------


sb3 BATHS                                      7

---------------------------/ GUY:


GUY I/V                         Another of London's old Victorian

                                swimming baths is due to close.

                                Tower Hamlets Council say that the

                                Whitechapel baths in the East End

                                are  uneconomical  and  are  used

                                largely by city workers rather than

                                local people.  But regular users

                                of the pool are protesting and

                                don't think the prospect of a new

                                leisure pool in Bethnal Green is

                                any consolation.  Tasneem Siddiqi

                                reports.


VT (BATHS)                      VT: (BATHS)

ASTONS                          IN:  "The Whitechapel....."

@ 1'27"  Councillor JEREMY SHAW

         Bethnal Green

         Neighbourhood  Committee


                                OUT: "....pulling the plug."


                                DUR:  2'22"
```

# Specimen: Sports Programme

```
                                        GRANDSTAND   (c)  BBC
GRANDSTAND INTRO:                        No shot numbers
3.6.85                                   cut lines in front of dialogue -
                                         Sports Department style.

VTR (HEX)                               /OPENING TITLES

                                         Out:  Music                    DUR:  44"

MIX TO SLIDEFILE                        /Tonight in front of millions of TV viewers and
+ " TAPE ROCKY
(rec. 1000)                              the 22,000 fans lucky enough to be at Loftus Road,
(2-shot)
MIX TO SLIDEFILE                        /Barry McGuigan attempts to fulfil his dream and
(rec. 1000)
(CU)                                     become Featherweight Champion of the World.

MIX TO VTR (HEX)   SOUND ONLY           /McGUIGAN QUOTE
                                         Out:  "...those £100 seats".        DUR:
                                               + laugh

MIX TO VT-10                            /MUSICAL ITEM

                                         Out:  "...music".                   DUR:

MIX TO VTR (HEX)                        /ad lib
BOB OOV.




                                         And you'll be able to see the whole of that

                                         world title fight, Pedroza against McGuigan,

                                         live on BBC-1 tonight at 9.40

MIX GRAPHICS                            /That's tonight and on Grandstand this afternoon
BOB OOV.
                                         more international sport at the highest level.

TURN TO VT-10            14"            /From Paris, the French Open Championships, the
TENNIS
BOB OOV.                                 Ladies' Singles Final and that long running double

(W/A - 5")                               bill.  There's the world's No. 1 Martina
(CU Navratilova + A/A - 9")
                                         Navratilova, who completed the Grand Slam in Paris

                                         last year, a feat which entitled her to a little

                                         bonus of 1,000,000 dollars.
                                         SOVT:  Out:                         DUR:
(CU Lloyd)              4"               Martina's opponent for the 65th time - Chris Lloyd,

                                         the world's No. 2.
                                         SOVT:  Out: "...that's the bottom line"  DUR: 30"
```

```
                              6/            ┌─────────────────────┐
                    /3, 4, 1, 5, 2/         │ TOP OF THE POPS     │
                                            │ (c) BBC             │
                    AREA A                  │                     │
                                            │ Pop music script    │
                    JIM DIAMOND             │ showing split bars  │
                                            │ and beats           │
                                            └─────────────────────┘

                    "HI HO SILVER"                (3'50")

                    (Jim Diamond/Chris Parren=MCPS/BIEM/
                    Rondor Music (London) Ltd./Most
                    Music Publ. Co. Ltd.)

                    /CAM 4 FED TO EID/        /Q APPLAUSE/
                                             /Q TRACK/


                    1,2,3          (SLOW TEMPO)

                    Sometimes I sit here

                    feeling alone

                    No one to talk to
        MIX
  2.    1           I got no telephone /
        LA WS SET + FORE-HEADS
                                       (CHANGE TEMPO)
                                    1 BAR
        S/I ASTON
          5.  JIM DIAMOND          And at night I wake up
              "Hi Ho Silver"
                                    1,2
        T/O ASTON
                                    I just lie and stare

  4.    4                          3,4/1,2,/        (5/2)
        MS JIM
                                    Come on and save me

  5.    6                          from this nightmare / (1/2)
        MS DRUMMER & KIT
  6.    5                          3,4/1,2 /
        LS JIM

  7.    2                          Hi Ho Silver/
        M2-S BRASS                 3,4/1,2
  8.    4                                /
        MCU JIM                    Here comes the Lone Ranger
  9.    2                                           /
        CS BRASS A/B               3,4/1,2
 10.    1                                /
        FS JIM & BAND              He's riding on down
        ELEVATE & TIGHTEN
        TO MLS JIM                 3,4/1,2
        (2 next)
```

# Specimen Conventional Drama Script

```
                                        DOCTOR WHO  (c)  BBC
                                        standard drama layout

( 163  on 1)              - 1/23 -                      (48)
                                                       & 49


   164.  2        C/S        THE DOCTOR:  What? /
                  DASTARI

                             DASTARI:      Hasn't it
                             occurred to you that the
                             Time Lords have a vested
                             interest in insuring
                             that others do not
   165.  1        C/S        discover their secrets?  /
                  DOCTOR

                             THE DOCTOR:  I'm sure
   166.  2        C/S        that's not the case.  /
                  DASTARI

                             DASTARI:      I gather your
                             own machine is no longer
                             in the station.  Isn't
                             that because you didn't
                             want Kartz and Reimer
   167.  5        2S         to get a look at it?  /
                  JAMIE b/gL
                  DR.f/gR
                             THE DOCTOR:  Look, I've a
                             suggestion.  Stop these
                             experiments for the time
                             being while my people
   168.  1        C/S        study their work./  If
                  DOCTOR     Kartz and Reimer are
                             really on safe lines I'm
                             sure they'll be allowed
   169.  2        2/S        to continue./
                  DASTARI over
                  DR.T'S L.sh
                  Pan up as DASTARI  DASTARI:      Allowed to
                  rises              continue?

                  T.O.L. panning
                  DASTARI R to top   THE DOCTOR:  I mean there
                  of aisle with      would be no further
                  JAMIE R of him     objection.
                  to 3S
                             DASTARI:      In the first
                             place I have no authority
                             to ask Kartz and Reimer
                             to submit their work for
                             analysis.  And in the
                             second place, the Time
                             Lords have no right to
                             make such a grossly
                             unethical demand.  I've
                             never heard such unmitigated
   170.  1        M/S        arrogance!/
                  DOCTOR
                  Pan him L
   (5 next)       to 3S
```

# Specimen: Situation Comedy, Non-Standard

|  |  |  | NO PLACE LIKE HOME (c)  BBC |
|---|---|---|---|

preferred layout for L.E. shows
not liked by PA's and vision
mixers.  Cut lines cause
confusion.

- 45 -

(Shot 120 on 3)

---

121.   4   M.S. BERYL

BERYL.
Yes ... that's what I thought.

Do you ... um ...want us to leave?

---

122.   3   2-SHOT
ARTHUR/ABIGAIL

ARTHUR.
Oh come on Beryl, no.  We were

just...er...finishing.

---

123.   2   M.C.U. ABIGAIL

ABIGAIL.
I think your husband is very good

Mrs. Crabtree.  He ought to do

more of it.

---

124.   5   M.C.U. TREVOR

TREVOR.
I bet he'd like to.  (GRINS)

---

125.   2   M.C.U. ABIGAIL

ABIGAIL.
I think he has got talent.

---

126.   5   M.C.U. TREVOR

TREVOR.
He likes a bit of talent.  (SMIRKS)

---

127.   3   2-SHOT
ARTHUR/ABIGAIL

ARTHUR.
(PEEVED)  Did you want something

Trevor?

---

(4 NEXT)

# Specimen: Unscripted Magazine Programme

```
                                        SATURDAY SUPERSTORE (c) BBC
                                        More like a detailed running
                                        order than a standard script -
                                        but it works!

                             SATURDAY SUPERSTORE
                                   22.2.86.

09.00.00                     SEQ 1


                             WAREHOUSE                    (0'30")
4: SIEVEHEAD

3: 2-S                       CROW/SIEVEHEAD

CU SIEVEHEAD                 SIEVEHEAD    (BEEPS)


2-S                          CROW:

                             OK what's going on?


CU SIEVEHEAD                 SIEVEHEAD:   (BEEPS)


2-S                          CROW:

                             Ok.  What is the brand new show you've

                             got for us?

                                                   FX

                                        /DRUM ROLL/


                             SIEVEHEAD

CU GRAPHIC                   BEEPS AND PULLS CURTAIN TO REVEAL GRAPHIC



                             CROW:

                             The sievehead Show?  I don't think so!

                             We'll stick to Saturday Superstore.

09.00.30   VT SEQ A          _____


                             OPENING TITLES:

                             IN:
```

# Specimen: Multi-Pass Electronic Layout

<u>GALLACTIC GARDEN</u> (c)  BBC
example of CSO multi pass
layout


BLUE AREA.   DB ON KIRBY WIRE


A GRASSHOPPER ON THE GROUND,
CHEWING WHAT IT CHEWS.  DB FALLS
INTO SHOT BESIDE IT AND, STARTLED,
IT JUMPS AWAY.


6.  <u>TK_____</u>          <u>DAVE</u>   (FALLS, ARMS ABOVE HIS HEAD
        Grasshopper                   AND BRINGS THEM DOWN WHEN
                                      HE HITS THE GROUND TAKING A
                                      COUPLE OF STEPS ON THE SPOT
                                      AS IF REGAINING HIS BALANCE.
    O/L                               WHEN GRASSHOPPER HAS GONE,
    <u>2_____</u>        DB TAKES TWO STEPS SCREEN
        WS DB on kirby wire           LEFT)

    <u>/FX INLAY DESK MASK/</u>          Thank goodness it's only a grasshopper,
    <u>/TO PUT DB BEHIND/</u>
    <u>/BLADE OF GRASS/</u>            for they are vegetarian.


    TILT DB into shot
    thru top of frame
    and settle him on
    ground beside
    grasshopper


<u>/RECORDING BREAK/</u>

# Specimen: Script for Multi-Vocal Opera

```
                                    COSI FAN TUTTI  (c)  BBC
                    (-17-)  - 9 -   example of multi-vocal layout

                              DAYS 1/2 : 25TH/26TH SEPT.

                                  ACT 1 : Scene 4


(NO.6  QUINTET  cont.)                                      (p.48)

(on 2 : 5/s)          ┌ FIORD./DORAB.
                      │ So does Fate take away the joy of living
                      │
                      │ FERR.
                      │       Gone is all the joy of living,
                      │
                      │ GUGL./D.ALF
                      │            So the sudden hand of Fate
                      └      will take away the joy of living


                      ┌ FIORD./DORAB.
                      │ End forever all the hopes and dreams we
                      │                               cherished
                      │ FERR.
                      │       all----the hopes and dreams we
                      │                           cherished
                      │
                      │ GUGL./D.ALF.
                      │        So the sudden hand of Fate will
                      └      take away the joy of living

                        ALL:
                        Bowed by grief, alone in sorrow,
                        Who would care to live at all,
                        Who? Who? Who?  Who?
                        Who would care to live at all

Shots 12-15           ┌ FIORD.
                      │        Ah-- who would care to live
CUT-INS, as directed  │                          at all
                      │ DORAB.
                      │ Who would care, who would care to live
                      │                          at all,
                      │ FERR.
                      │        Who would care to live
                      │                          at all,
                      │ GUGL./D.ALF.
                      │ Yes,  who would care to live
                      └                    at all,

                      ┌ FIORD.
                      │        Ah-- who would care to live
                      │                            at all,
                      │ DORAB.
                      │  Who would care, who would care to live
                      │                            at all,
                      │ FERR.
                      │ Who would,   who would care to live
                      │                            at all,
                      │ GUGL./D.ALF.
                      │  Yes,    who would   care to live
                      └                          at all,
```

# Specimen: Magazine Programme Running Order

```
                                        ┌─────────────┐
                                        │ GOING LIVE! │
                                        │ (c) BBC     │
                                        └─────────────┘
GOING LIVE!        RUNNING ORDER        SATURDAY 18 NOVEMBER 1989

TIME      AREA/CAMS              SEQ/PAGE/ITEM          DUR

09.09.00  DESK                   SEQ 4/P9               4'00

          3: PHILLIP/CU's        GORDON/PHILLIP

          4: 2s                  PHILLIP MENTIONS
                                 CHILDREN IN NEED/
          5: GORDON              GIVES NUMBERS/
                                 READS LETTERS/
                                 LOOKS AT BORING
                                 POSTCARDS/GIVES
                                 ADDRESS

-------------------------------------------------------------

09.13.00                         VT: JOKES              1'00

-------------------------------------------------------------

09.14.00  MITZI AREA             SEQ 5/P11              4'00

          1: SARAH               SARAH (CAM R OF MONITOR)

          2: SARAH + MONITOR     SHOWS STARSHOT WAVE/LINES
                                 NOW CLOSED/RECAPS GAME/
                                 SHOWS PRIZES/PLAYS STARSHOT/
                                 TRAILS MORE LATER/LINKS TO
                                 BLACK ADDER CLIP

-------------------------------------------------------------

09.18.00                         VT: BLACK ADDER
                                     /MAID MARION       2'00

-------------------------------------------------------------

09.20.00  DEMO                   SEQ 6/P13              3'00

          1: TONY                PHILLIP/TONY ROBINSON

          2: 2s                  CHAT/TRAIL CALLS/LINK
                                 TO KISSYFUR PART 1

          3: PHILLIP

          1: L2s (INC
             PHONE AREA)
-------------------------------------------------------------

09.23.00                         VT: KISSYFUR PART 1    11'00
                                     "EVILFUR"

          (REH SISTER BROS SEQ 8)

          (REH TRAIL SEQ 10)
-------------------------------------------------------------
```

# Specimen: Current Affairs
# Running Order

```
NEWSROOM SOUTH EAST RUNNING ORDER:        Wednesday 28th February
EDITOR:...........                        DIRECTOR:..............

------------------------------------------------------------------

1.   (ti) TITLES              CAM 3           w/s
                              CAM 2           GUY
                              VT              (opening titles)
                              VT              (headlines)

2.   (db) ROADS REPORT        CAM 2 w/s       GUY + monitors
                              VT              (roads report)

3.   (bm) ARCADE TRIAL        CAM 2 MCU       GUY
                              VT              (archade trial)
                              CAM 1 MCU       DAVID ARCHER + aston

4.   (dh) INNER CITIES        CAM 2 MCU       GUY
                              VT              (Inner cities)

5.        NEWS                CAM 3 MCU       GUY hands to ROB
                              CAM 1 MCU       ROB CURLING + aston
                              STILLS STORE
                              VTs             separate sheet

6.   (rg) NATIONAL TRUST      CAM 2 w/s       GUY + monitors
                              VT              (National Trust)

7.   (fw) LEGO                CAM 2 MCU       GUY
                              CAM 3           props on desk
                              VT              (lego)
                              CAM 1 MCU       ALAN MURRAY + aston

8.        WEATHER & TRAVEL    CAM 2 MCU       GUY
                              CAM 3           GUY hands to ROB
                              CAM 1 MCU       ROB
                              STILLS STORE

9.   (cl) CLOSE               CAM 2 MCU       GUY
                              CAM 3           w/s
                              CART + aston    (back at 9.25)
                              LIGHTS

------------------------------------------------------------------

STANDBYS:

1.   SE heads
2.   Address
3.   Poster address
4.   History trail
5.   College          (2'08")
6.   Secret Cinema    (3'01")
7.   hunting          (1'54")
```

# CAMERA CARDS

Cameramen do not use scripts as they need both hands free to operate their cameras. Their information is given on camera cards, each one being an extract of the shot numbers from the camera script relevant to a particular camera, giving descriptions of the shot and moves and positions for the various shots. There should always be sufficient room on the card for the cameraman to add his own notes.

As the cameramen listen to the PA shot calling, they have immediate reference on their camera card to where they are on the script, what shot they have to get next and what position they need to be in to get it.

Do remember to leave lots of space on the card for the cameraman's notes. Don't put too many shots on each card.

```
CAMERA: 1          Title:

SHOT    POS.   DESCRIPTION                    NOTES


                SC. 6  INT. LOUNGE. DAY 2      2A   4B


  51      A     MS ANNE

                TIGHTEN TO
                MCU


  53            MCU ANNE


  55            MS ANNE + EXIT

                Z/O TO WS LOUNGE
                INC. ROSS
```

## Numbers of cards for different types of cameras

The standard studio camera 'ped' takes one card with holes punched at the top, but many a PA has been caught out by the different numbers of cards required and the different types of clips used to attach the card to the camera.

The extra cards are for the other members of the crew who need to push or steer the camera mounting. Most of the cards will be mounted on a clipboard with holes at the top of the card. OB cameras often have side mountings for cards, or no clips at all, so sellotape or bull dog clips might be required for these.

If various types of camera mountings are being discussed at the planning meeting, make sure the designer knows, not least because some of them need a considerable amount of studio floor space in which to operate. Also, certain mountings used to provide very high studio shots will require the cameraman to wear a hard hat.

| CAMERA | NUMBER/SIZE OF CARD |
|---|---|
| Ikegami (small handheld) | 1/4 |
| Ped (standard studio cam) | 1 |
| Heron | 2 |
| Creeper | 2 |
| Vlad (for low shots) | 2 |
| Mole Crane | 3 |
| Nike | 4 |
| Chapman titan | 10 |

# Chapter 13

# The Role of the PA on Location

# PART III

The PA's role can take you anywhere. Some prefer a warm cosy studio, others yearn for the great outdoors.

Until recently most location shooting was on film, but more and more productions are turning to video to record their material. It does, however, depend on the nature of the programme material as to which format is used.

The PA's task of noting the material shot is very similar whatever format is used, so whether you are recording the shots identified by a film clapperboard or a video counter, the only variation is likely to be the paperwork.

The planning stages may also vary slightly, but whatever the format, you will still find yourself going on location recces, arranging accommodation, taking the kitchen sink with you and getting wet!

This chapter will concentrate on documentary filming and all the implications of a film location shoot. However, a lot of the detail regarding planning and preparation will cross reference with Chapter 14 on *Outside Broadcasts*, so anyone about to embark on a programme with a location element would do well to read both chapters.

But first a few words about other types of programme location work (details appear in the relevant specialist chapters) along with some of the less obvious tasks that you could end up doing.

**Magazine inserts**

News and current affairs inserts are now nearly always shot on video. They tend to be 'on-the-day' shoots and need a fast, electronically-edited turn round for transmission, without the delays involved in film processing.

Less urgent material — for example a weekly magazine pro-gramme — may be recorded on either format, with video increasingly preferred, to match the picture quality of the studio shots for ease of editing into the final version.

## Drama

Depending on the location, some drama shoots will be on single camera, either film or video. Others will stretch to a mini two-camera unit or a full-scale outside broadcast scanner. But, shooting half-way up a mountain or down a pothole is much simpler on film, which does not require cables that trail back to electronic equipment.

## Documentaries

Documentaries are usually shot on film, for flexibility in editing. The format of the programme is less precise than a scripted drama and shots will be 'gathered' from many locations and then edited with flexibility in the film cutting room.

## Crowd control

Many a PA has had to abandon her shot list to keep a crowd from gathering in the street. Where do those awful people come from waving scarves and arms in the back of the shot? A little bluff can usually stall them from too much offensive behaviour and the hollow promise of an interview can keep even the most persistent individual at bay long enough to get what you want recorded.

## Catering

You may well be expected to provide teas and coffees on locations (although this is traditionally the AFM's task). On smaller productions without the luxury of an AFM, it is likely to fall to the PA. Your canteen should be able to supply thermos flasks and tins of biscuits.

## First aid

On location you could well be called upon to supply an aspirin or sticking plaster. However, don't take on any medical problems that you do not feel competent to deal with. Larger productions have production managers or stage managers who are responsible for health and safety.

# DOCUMENTARY FILMING

Documentary or factual filming is an umbrella title covering everything except drama and music. Previous chapters in this book have covered budgeting and setting up a programme so, we'll start here with the recce.

### The recce

The term recce comes from the word *reconnoitre* which means an examination or survey, scouring, exploration. In production terms it's when a meeting is held on site to work out the logistics of filming and therefore ensure a trouble-free filming day. There may be more than one recce; a preliminary one where the director will visit a number of possible locations before making a decision, followed by a final, more detailed recce. The PA should attend, and if it is a complicated shoot, so should the cameraman.

For a number of reasons it is important that the PA attends at least the final recce — two heads are better than one. She will then be familiar with the location and able to answer queries both in the production office and on the actual day, thus easing the load on the director. When on the recce look at the location from a practical viewpoint. Ask yourself "what will be required on and for the day?" Remember you will be outside the safe confines of the office where most things are to hand.

### The location
* Note the full address and telephone number
* The owner's details
* The contact's details
* Directions — a hand drawn map may be required.

### Transport
* Car parking — how many production and crew cars will there be on the day?
* Mini bus — if filming at more than one location with limited parking (for example, Central London), it may be more practical to hire a transit van and driver.

**Refreshments**
- Meals, coffee, tea, etc
- Where?

**Toilets**
- Where are they? What condition are they in?
- Are they for your exclusive use or are they for the general public?
- Will you have to arrange for a company to supply them?

**Hazards**
- Tides, low-flying aircraft, unguarded heights, dangerous substances, etc.

### Street filming

Contact local police station, giving full details of the proposed filming. Note the contact's name for future reference.

If the police are not informed they have every right to stop you filming, because crowds appear from nowhere when filming in the streets, and the police consider it a hazard to safety. You may need extra help to deal with on-lookers.

### Setting up

Once back from the recce and in the production office details need to be finalised and confirmed and the film crew booked.

### Put it in writing

Confirmation letters and contracts need to be sent to contributors and locations detailing the requirements and breakdown of the day.

### Accommodation

If you need to stay overnight, book and confirm production accommodation — special rates may be negotiated if you are a sizeable party. Film crews usually make their own arrangements but this should be checked.

### The film crew

A standard documentary crew is three people — cameraman, assistant and sound recordist. Some documentary assignments, especially those involving actors or musicians, will require extra staff such as a sound assistant to cope with extra microphones, and film grips who will rig extra equipment and lay track. If interior shooting is planned, lights will be required along with a number of lighting operators. The cameraman can advise you about the correct number of people for the shoot.

### Equipment

When booking the crew, you may need to book additional equipment as well. There will be a standard set of equipment including the obvious gear, such as the camera, as well as a variety of lenses and filters. Check with your film manager if you think extra equipment may be required.

### Film stock and film sound

You will need to make sure that enough stock is taken with you for filming. Filming ratios can vary enormously depending on the type of filming and are affected by whether the story is scripted or unscripted, by the approach of an organised and economic director and by the "grab anything we might use" school of directorial extravagance.

### Camera and sound rolls

A camera roll is four hundred feet long and lasts for approximately ten minutes. The sound roll lasts for twenty minutes. Note down on the shot list each time a new roll is started, if required. The usual gauge for documentary filming is 16mm and there are two types of film:

NEGATIVE STOCK: (e.g. Eastman Colour). As suggested by its name, the film is negative after processing. From this negative, positive copies can be struck. The editor works on the positive copy, keeping the original negative untouched until the answer and showprints are produced at the labs.

REVERSAL STOCK: (e.g. Ektachrome). After processing, the film gives a positive image. There is no negative, the editor cuts the original film, which is transmitted. This stock is mainly used for programmes with a fast turn around, such as a nightly current affairs programme which has not yet switched to video.

The sound is recorded on (usually) a Nagra recorder which uses quarter-inch magnetic tape with a governing 'pulse' that corresponds to the sprocket holes on the film. After filming, this tape is transferred to 16mm magnetic film, (called the mag track) and cassette copies can also be made at this stage.

Discuss all the details of the shoot with the Film Office or the film hire company. They will be able to advise you on extra equipment requirements together with the best scheduling of the shoot — although this should be for the director to decide.

**Crew hours**

Crews work to standard days and extra charges will be made to the production for late/short meal breaks and overtime. Remember that the cost soon mounts up when each penalty is multiplied by the number of crew members. So be fully versed on the rules and practices which govern the hours of work, in order to schedule the crew economically and effectively.

**Film schedule**

The film schedule is the blueprint for the filming day. It should be clear and comprehensive combining the information gathered from the recce together with the breakdown of the filming days. Distribute this as soon as you can, it may highlight problem areas (see the example on page 122).

**Distribution:**
- Film Office or hire company (including crew's copies)
- Production team, production file, production office — door, desk
- Contributors Location
- Spares to take on location

# Specimen: Film Schedule

FILM SCHEDULE                                    COSTING NUMBER

PROGRAMME TITLE

FILMING DATES

```
        Producer ...............................
        Director ...............................
        PA .....................................

        Film Cameraman .........................
        Assistant Cameraman ....................
        Sound Recordist ........................
        Lights .................................

                        * * * *
        Presenter ..............................

                        * * * *
```

NOTES

```
1)  Special equipment
2)  Lab details
3)  Sound transfer details - transcription copies
4)  Board information
5)  Useful numbers - facilities house, police, base
6)  Production hotel accommodation
7)  Travel information
8)  Special clothing
```

# Specimen: Shooting Schedule

- 2 -

<u>SHOOTING SCHEDULE</u>

| Time | RV - Production & Crew | Location<br>Contact<br>Telephone Number<br>Directions<br>Parking |
|------|------------------------|-----------------|
| Time | SHOOT | Details - interior/<br>exterior<br>- g/vs/ptc/<br>interviews |
| Time | TRAVEL TO | Location |
| Time | LUNCH/WRAP | |

<u>SPECIAL NOTES</u>

Any notes re locations e.g. no smoking, keep gates shut, passes, etc.

Brief summary of programme/shoot.

<u>ATTACH</u>

Maps of locations with arrow marking <u>exact</u> site.

## Clothing

Be practical about clothing on location and dress according to the situation. One rule that applies to whatever you are filming — comfortable shoes — remember you'll be on your feet most of the day.

If you are filming out-of-doors — nine times out of ten it will be wet — so keep the waterproofs handy. Layers of clothing are the order of the day for filming both exteriors and interiors, so garments can be shed or added.

If your location requires special clothing, e.g. strong shoes or walking boots for rocky terrains, do warn everybody. This information should go on the film schedule.

When filming business functions, formal occasions or royalty — don't turn up in jeans. You may well find you need to dress quite formally, so check on etiquette with the venue as some of them spring surprises — golf clubs, for instance, can insist on formal attire. In short, don't wear a frock and high heels for filming down a pothole and don't wear jeans and a scruffy anorak for Buckingham Palace. Use a little commonsense and you can't go far wrong.

## Cash

On many productions, the PA is responsible for the production purse. Don't take your own money, always take out a cash advance. Check exactly what you will be responsible for — in some cases, this could include the contributors' and crew's expenses. Some artists' expenses also have to be paid out whilst away on location.

If you are away for a long time, make arrangements with a local bank. Always over-estimate the amount you are going to need and be prepared for all contingencies.

Keep a notebook logging all expenditure on location and keep receipts, you will never remember everything when it comes to filling out your expenses claims in the office.

## Packing list

The following list will of, course, be dependent upon the length and type of shoot:

Shot list pad/notebook

Clipboard/file

Stopwatch

| | |
|---|---|
| Mini stationery store | Pens, pencils, rubber, ruler, headed and plain paper, compliment slips, envelopes, carbon paper, stamps. |
| Facility fee pads or letters | These are to cover small payments e.g. facilities, contributors, any situation where there's no receipt. They will also provide copyright of any interviews or vox pops recorded away from base. |
| Confirmation letters | Copies are advisable. |
| Large plastic bag | If it rains, shot list can be written under cover. |
| Typewriter | Investigate possibility of using the hotel's? |
| Maps | Both official and home produced where necessary. |
| Thermos flask | If no facilities are available at the location go prepared with flasks and tea, coffee and sugar. |
| Address book | |
| Cash | |

## On location

Once on location there are likely to be a couple of rehearsals whatever the shot to allow the cameraman and sound recordist to check that they can accommodate the action. If there is to be a piece to camera from a presenter, there may be a run through, so there should be enough time for you to sort out what is about to happen. Once the camera, sound and artists are ready, filming begins.

## Who says what on location...

| | |
|---|---|
| QUIET PLEASE | Director or production manager |
| GOING FOR A TAKE | Director or production manager |
| STAND BY | Director or production manager |
| BOARD IN | Cameraman |
| TURN OVER | Director |
| CAMERA RUNNING | Cameraman |
| SOUND RUNNING/SPEED | Sound recordist |
| MARK IT | Cameraman |
| ACTION/CUE | Director or production manager |
| CUT | Director |

## Where to stand

When the filming starts, it is best to stand behind the camera for two reasons. Firstly, you won't be in the shot and, secondly, because the shot description should be from the camera's point of view, e.g. for someone walking in or out of shot, or eyelines.

Whilst filming, the PA's role will encompass countless tasks from taking the shot list, to public relations, from runner to clapperboard operator. You are there to ensure the day runs smoothly and all the filming is achieved.

## Taking a shot list

The director's requirements of a shot list will vary, so do check exactly what is wanted beforehand. Also work out your system for taking a shot list. Are you going to use pre-printed pads in a file or on a clipboard, a shorthand notebook or a lined pad?

If you are working on film, note the slate number; if on video, note the time code.

For each shot you should note the shot size, duration, in and out cues of any speech, questions and continuity.

## Working out the shot sizes

The director will usually discuss the shot with the cameraman so, by listening, you will be able to gather a lot of the required information.

With experience you will be able to work out the shot size from the lens on the camera and the position of the zoom handle (if used). The camera assistant will help you out with this. With the cameraman's permission you might also look down the eyepiece of the camera to check the shot size so that you can write it accurately in your notes.

## End boards

Sometimes a shot is idented at the end and the clapperboard is then held upside down. This may be for surreptitious filming. However, it takes twice as long to sync up an end board and is therefore not popular in the cutting room. Write EB by the shot number if an end board has been used. It will be assumed to be a front board unless otherwise stated.

## Mute boards

If there is no sound, a mute board is used for visual identi-fication. This is when the clapstick is either held open or kept closed.

## Good and no good takes

Make a note if the take was good or no good and the reason why. Many editors say there is no such thing as a 'No Good Take', so it is always very important to say why you went for another take. Either sound or picture may well be used in the final product.

### Timing for documentary shoots

Timing of the shot should be from ACTION to CUT. However, it is advisable to start the stopwatch with the command TURN-OVER and to flick it back on ACTION. This is to ensure the click of starting the watch isn't picked up by sound. It might well be worth muffling your stopwatch in a pocket.

### Continuity

Don't forget continuity when you are on a documentary. Some people think it is even more difficult than in drama, as there is no formal script other than the text, and sometimes nothing more than an elaborate running order.

A broader look at continuity is contained in Chapter 16. Briefly, if a person is in shot you should be aware of continuity — i.e. jacket open or buttoned up, glasses — and any action (e.g. pointing or turning) which must be matched in different shots.

### Entering and leaving frame

To ensure movement continues in the same direction, always note which side of shot an artist enters or leaves. If he leaves camera right he must re-enter camera left. If he enters shot camera right he will have made a U-turn.

### Interviews

At some stage or other in a documentary shoot, you are likely to come across an interview situation. As you will be shooting this with one camera, you need to note a few things whilst filming the interviewee, before you set up the camera again to film the interviewer (the reverse).

• **Eyelines** have to be noted to ensure the interviewer and interviewee are looking at each other when the film is cut together. If you have difficulty in working out eyelines draw a diagram showing the position of the camera, the interviewer and interviewee or little diagrams of the shots — a simple circle with a nose says it all.

- **Questions** — shorthand is useful here. Errors are often made when the question is not taken down accurately and when it is repeated for the reverse question, it doesn't match with the interviewee's response.

- **Summary of answer** — note possible cutaways (subjects which can be filmed later and used to illustrate the answer).

## Crossing the line

The 'line' is an imaginary one drawn between two objects being filmed. As long as the camera stays on the same side of the line the 'geography' of the shot will be correct. In an interview the line would be between the interviewer and interviewee. Sketches and diagrams are often useful to keep track of eyelines.

## Your other roles when on location

Shot listing is only one of the roles on location. You can often find yourself acting as the link between the director and the crew. It is far from being an ideal situation, but it is most important that relationships on location remain amicable to benefit both the working atmosphere and the work itself.

Sometimes you could well be wearing your public relations hat — soothing nervous interviewees, keeping members of the public, who seem to be drawn to filming like magnets, at bay and quiet — while still trying to do your other jobs.

## There's never enough time

Always keep an eye on the schedule and inform the director if you are running over and the implications of this. If it looks as though you might arrive late at the next location, ring and inform your contact there — keep everyone informed. If major changes to the schedule occur, relay these to the production office.

At the end of the day, the camera assistant and sound recordist will despatch the film and sound rolls to be processed. On a fast turn round for transmission, some film editors want some kind of shot list included with the rushes, whilst others are happy to wait for a neat copy in a few days time.

### Leave the location tidy

Do make sure the location is left as you found it — tidy. Many second attempts to visit a location have been refused because it was left in a mess the first time.

It is very tempting, especially when a production is behind schedule, to move on quickly to the next location, without checking that all is as you found it. It may well fall to you if there is no AFM, to collect all the rubbish in dustbin sacks and take those away with you for disposal elsewhere.

### Contributors

Double check you have the correct spelling and title for all the programme's contributors, for name supers in the edited version. Also, take addresses for thank you letters and to enable you to contact them when a transmission date has been finalised.

# POST FILMING

Once back in the office the paperwork element looms.

### Shot lists

The shot list needs to be typed up — see example on p.131. (This can sometimes be aided/checked with a VHS of the rushes). It is used as a reference document by the director and film editor and should be a clear, concise record of the filming.

Headings (e.g. locations, interviews) can be used as signposts. Continuity notes made on location should not be included, as they were for your benefit to ensure different shots will cut together — the editor will be able to see if the cuts work or not.

# Specimen: Shot List (Film)

```
Programme title:................Costing number:.........

Filming dates

Producer:..........Director:...........Film Editor:.........

Cameraman:.........Sound recordist:.....Presenter:...........
```

| Cam Roll No | Slate No | Take | Description | Sound | Tape No | Dur |
|---|---|---|---|---|---|---|
| | | | ALDENHAM COUNTRY PARK | | | |
| 1 | 1 | 1 | LS avenue of trees | S | 1 | 32" |
| | 2 | 1 | ws reservoir - PAN R across wood ending on CU trunk of fir tree | S | | 43" |
| | 3 | 2 | Cu fir tree roots | M | | 18" |
| | 4 | 1 | Cu log zoom out to ws log pile | M | | 29" |
| | 5 | 1 | INTERVIEW - Peter Grey Tree warden | | | |
| | | | o/s 2s fav Peter, z/o to MCU over 2nd question | | | |
| | | | Q1: "How many trees have been damaged?" A: "Approx. 400 - third of park's trees." Q2: "Were gales worst in your experience?" A: "Worst in memory." | S | | 1'26" |
| | 6 | 1 | MCU presenter - noddies and reverse questions | S | | 52" |
| | 6 | 2 | Repeat Q2 - better | S | | 16" |
| 2 | 7eb | 1 | Establishing long 2s presenter/Peter Grey | S | | 12" |
| | 8 | 1 | GVs and cut-aways | M | | 46" |
| | 9 | 1 | CU robin on branch pull focus to sign on wall NB - too fast | S | | 48" |
| | 9 | 2 | A/B good | S | | 47" |
| | | | Wildtrack - atmos | | | |

# Specimen: Time Code Log (Video)

| PICTURE | IN | OUT | OK TAKE | DUR |
|---|---|---|---|---|
| bars | 00.00.00.00 | 02.00.00.00 | - | |
| LS avenue of trees | 02.00.30.00 | 02.01.02.16 | 1 | 32" |
| WS reservoir PAN R across wood ending on CU trunk of fir tree | 02.01.32.18 | 02.02.15.10 | 1 | 43" |
| CU fir tree roots | 02.04.16.12 | 02.04.34.06 | 2 | 18" |
| CU log z/out to WS log pile | 02.06.24.13 | 02.06.53.00 | 1 | 29" |
| INTERVIEW Peter Grey | 02.08.35.00 | 02.10.05.12 | 1 | 1'26" |
| noddies and reverses stop/start | 02.12.10.15 | 02.15.30.00 | 1 | 52" |
| Q2 again | 02.17.30.10 | 02.18.00.14 | 2 | 16" |
| establishing long 2s pres+int | 02.25.30.16 | 02.26.15.15 | 1 | 12" |
| GVs & C/As | 02.27.00.12 | 02.35.16.02 | 1 | - |
| CU robin on branch pull focus to sign on wall | 02.37.02.15 | 02.39.14.07 | 2 | 48" |
| extra GVs for wildtrack sound in edit | 02.40.00.00 | 02.43.00.00 | 1 | - |

## Transcripts

Transcripts of interviews and pieces to camera may be required. Often they can be sent out to transcription typists but, in that case, do detail precisely which shots are to be transcribed.

Copies of both the shot list and transcript should be given to the director and editor and one set put in the programme file. The director may make an assembly order (editing script) from these two documents.

## Thank you letters

Thank you letters with transmission details, if appropriate and known, should be sent to all the contributors. Never lead people to believe that they will be included in the final film if you feel that there is any doubt.

# THE EDITING PROCESS

## Rushes and sound transfer

The film will have been processed overnight and the rushes (ungraded colour print) are viewed for technical quality. The sound tape has been transferred to 16mm magnetic tape. A sound cassette may also be useful.

## Syncing up and rubber numbering

The rushes are then sunc-up and rubber numbered (known as limited editing) to ensure the picture and corresponding sound can be matched up.

## The rough cut to fine cut

The editor will then translate the director's assembly order into a rough cut — the first assembly — which is then further edited into the fine cut.

# Specimen: Dubbing Sheet

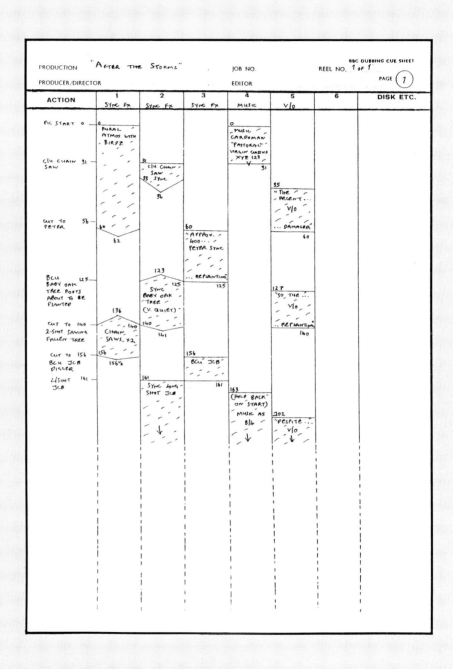

| PRODUCTION "AFTER THE STORMS" | | | | JOB NO. | | | REEL NO. 1 OF 1 |
|---|---|---|---|---|---|---|---|
| PRODUCER/DIRECTOR | | | | EDITOR | | | PAGE 1 |

**BBC DUBBING CUE SHEET**

| ACTION | 1 SYNC FX | 2 SYNC FX | 3 SYNC FX | 4 MUSIC | 5 V/O | 6 | DISK ETC. |
|---|---|---|---|---|---|---|---|
| PIC START 0 | RURAL ATMOS WITH BIRDS | | | 0 MUSIC CARDOMAN "PASTORAL" VIRGIN CLASSICS XYE 123 31 | | | |
| C/U CHAIN 31 SAW | | 31 C/U CHAIN SAW SYNC 33 36 | | | 35 "THE RECENT... V/O ...DAMAGED" 60 | | |
| CUT TO 5b PETER | 60 62 | | 60 "APPROX. 400... PETER SYNC | | | | |
| BCU 125 BABY OAK TREE ROOTS ABOUT TO BE PLANTED | | 123 125 SYNC BABY OAK TREE (V. QUIET) | ...REPLANTING 125 | | 127 "SO THE... V/O ...REPLANTING 140 | | |
| CUT TO 140 2-SHOT SAWING FALLEN TREE | 136 140 CHAIN SAWS ×2 | 140 141 | | | | | |
| CUT TO 156 BCU JCB DIGGER | 156 156½ | | 156 BCU JCB | | | | |
| L/SHOT 161 JCB | | 161 SYNC LONG SHOT JCB | 161 | 163 (HOLD BACK ON START) MUSIC AS B/4 ↓ | 202 "DESPITE... V/O ↓ | | |

# Specimen: Commentary Script

AFTER THE STORMS

0035      The recent gales have taken their toll at Aldenham Country Park. Trees, fences, buildings in fact practically anything standing has been damaged. I asked Peter Grey, Tree Warden, how many trees have been damaged.

     IN:   "Approximately 400 trees..."

     OUT:  "...large scale replanting".

0127      So the park workers have a heavy work schedule ahead of them - clearing the fallen trees, repairing and replanting.

0202      Despite all the devastation there are signs that Sporing is only just around the corner.

### Track laying

Once the editing is completed, track laying begins. This is the process of building up different sound tracks prior to the dub. Do keep in touch with and visit the cutting room whenever possible to see the various stages. Make a note and clear copyright, if applicable, of any music or footage obtained for the film editor.

### The commentary script

The commentary might be recorded before the dub. An example of a commentary script is shown on p.135.

### The dub

The dub is the final process of mixing and balancing of the sound tracks. Usually, a music and effects track (M&E) is mixed first and then the final mix is made. Be advised by the film editor on the amount of time required for the dub — with a lot of tracks they can take longer than expected.

### Neg cutting

The final stage for the film is neg cutting. The assistant film editor logs all the edge numbers on the completed film and from this log the film laboratories neg cut and produce an answerprint.

### The answerprint and showprint

This is a graded print and is examined by the director and/or film editor for colour and exposure. More than one answerprint may be struck, but once satisfactory a showprint is made. This can be transmitted or, more usually, transferred to VT for transmission.

### Post production script

A post-production script can be typed now, which will detail both the sound and visual content of the programme.

# FOREIGN FILMING

For foreign filming the same principles apply, together with extra considerations such as work permits, travel arrangements and innoculations. As the PA on a foreign assignment, you will probably be responsible for the co-ordination of these details for both production and crew. Above all, remember that the planning and organisation can take up a lot of your time, so start early.

### Permits/visas

Time is of the essence, especially where work permits are concerned so, as soon as the possibility of filming in a foreign country is raised, start researching immediately. The first point of contact is the Press Office of the Embassy or High Commission of the country concerned.

Ascertain whether work permits/visas are required, as these can take a very long time to be processed — a personal visit armed with all the necessary documents, passports and photographs can expedite the process.

### Passports

Passports can pose a problem if they contain stamps from countries not recognised or accepted by the country to be filmed in. In such cases a second 'clean' passport will need to be organised.

The Embassy/High Commission may well be able to furnish you with details of productions which have previously filmed in the country. It is well worth making contact to get advice and learn from others' experience.

### Innoculations

Check early with a doctor whether innoculations are required — remember some courses of injections can take six weeks. Ensure everyone has a medical certificate detailing all the innoculations as this too can be an entry requirement for some countries.

### Travel arrangements

If you have to make the travel arrangements, beware of charter/fixed flight bookings which, although cheaper than scheduled flights, eliminate flexibility and can end up more expensive if flights have to be altered.

### Money

The financial side also needs to be carefully organised. Over-estimate when calculating how much is needed — palms often need to be greased. For safety, take the majority in travellers cheques plus a small amount of local currency. Again, the use of a 'cash record' book is essential.

List all the travellers cheque numbers and details of encashment together with the exchange rate, as well as details of expenditure. This book becomes a log and expenses at the end of the trip will be fairly straightforward to compile. A number of credit cards can be arranged to cover hire cars, telephone calls and flights.

### Insurance

Health and personal effects insurance will need to be arranged for production and crew.

### Location information

Another point of contact will be the country's tourist board for accommodation and background information, e.g. climate, customs, public holidays, etc. Arm yourself with as much information, literature and maps as possible.

### Accommodation

Accommodation needs to be arranged. Again, depending on the size of the party, special rates may be negotiable.

Remember, if you are organising accommodation for the crew, a safe, secure storage space (possibly an extra bedroom) could be required for the equipment.

### The crew: British

If a British crew is booked, a *carnet* will be required. The *carnet* is a lengthy document for Customs which details every piece of equipment to be taken in and out of the country. The compilation of the *Carnet* is the responsibility of the cameraman and he may well have to charge a day's preparation time to the production.

Remember that the production is responsible for the crew's expenses when filming abroad.

### A helping hand through Customs

A shipping agent should be hired who will meet you and help to expedite your clearance through Customs. He will also organise the shipping back of the rushes.

### Excess baggage

If taking a British crew, equipment will mean a lot of excess baggage, so bear this in mind when booking the flights. Sometimes special deals can be arranged with airlines and many give discounts. Do remember always to reconfirm flights twenty-four hours prior to travelling.

### The crew: foreign

If you are hiring a crew in the foreign country, watch a few points. Firstly, are they of proven ability? If possible, get references from previous directors and view their work; secondly, do they use the British film standard (i.e. 25 frames per second) and have they a method of synchronising sound to the film. It may well be necessary to include a clapperboard on your packing list. Check also who is supplying the raw film stock and, if it is the crew, that it is of an acceptably high standard.

When working with a foreign crew make sure you know the details of their contract and how they are being paid. Find out if the rate includes daily subsistence allowances and travelling expenses.

### The packing list

The packing list will be dependent on the location and the type of filming to be undertaken. It is better to be safe than sorry, so pack for almost any contingency (see p.152).

Do take extra photocopies of all important documents — permits, licences, etc. They can often ease any difficult situation by being liberally distributed.

### Is your little off-the-shoulder number really suitable?

Do think carefully regarding clothing for foreign trips; there may be restrictions, where T-shirts and shorts are not permitted and in some countries you may also need headwear. If in doubt check with the tourist office.

### Anything and everything is your job when abroad

You could find yourself never seeing the actual filming whilst abroad, but acting more as a fixer. For instance, you may be left in the hotel each day to check up on the following day's arrangements and the shot list will have to be done in the cutting room once back home.

### Local helpers and interpreters

Local helpers and interpreters can be arranged; check with the local television company who will probably be able to provide you with all sorts of useful people and equipment: they can also be a valuable source of spare equipment, should anything break down.

# Chapter 14

# Outside Broadcasts

Outside Broadcasts will cover a large number of events ranging from sporting fixtures, in and out-of-doors such as golf and snooker tournaments which can go on for days, to a quick visit to the races. Also State and Parliamentary occasions, music concerts, both in the open air and in concert halls, ice shows, church services and dance championships; events such as air and boat shows, dog trials, special exhibitions, endurance contests and quiz programmes.

Many of the PA's jobs will be the same as those for similar programmes based in a studio, so refer to the chapters on drama, music and magazine programmes if your outside broadcast programme falls into one of those categories.

More and more drama location work is now being recorded on tape instead of film, either as a single-camera set up or with a multi-camera scanner, so refer to the drama and film chapters for more detail.

### Planning an OB

The main difference between an OB and a studio programme will be in the planning stages, plus a few extra details that have to be taken care of when away from base.

Once you know you are working on an OB, your director will begin to plan the logistics of the event. All the things you take for granted when at base become arrangements for you to make. Quite early in the proceedings the director will need to go on a recce to check out where the location is and what facilities are available. Go with him and make notes.

Obviously certain State occasions or sporting events will be regular fixtures on the OB calendar and previous requirements and bookings will probably be the same.

### Location contracts

Once a venue has been decided, do not discuss fees with anyone; let your location contracts department deal with this. There are standard contracts for the use of venues. If you are covering a sporting event, check up with the facilities department as some long-term contract may already exist. There may be 'shared' contracts, limiting you to certain dates for exclusive coverage of an event, although there can be some additional allowances for news.

The venue may well have been used before and a fee level set. If a very high fee is agreed (which your production might be able to afford, but which is unrealistic) a precedent could be set which would make it very expensive for other productions wishing to use the same venue in future.

## Planning meetings

When it comes to organising the planning meeting, it is important, if possible, to hold it at the venue. It then gives everyone involved a chance to see the problems first hand. It is important that the engineering manager and sound supervisor allocated to your production are present at the planning meeting.

Depending on the owner or organiser of the venue, it is certainly a courtesy to have them present at the meeting. Previous productions might well have tried things out that didn't work and the venue organisers do know their location better than anyone.

## Know your way round the venue

Take the opportunity whilst there to check out the layout of the venue. Is there a plan of the building available to include in the technical requirements? Get to know the organisers, and personnel, as they will prove very useful once into production, for such things as urgent photocopying.

## The technicalities

An engineering manager will be allocated to your production. On larger productions both an EM lighting and EM planning are allocated. The EM will arrange the technical matters, making sure that there is power available to run the OB unit or

— at large events, such as State occasions or golf tournaments — several scanners may be required. He will sort out where all the cables are to be laid and whether you will record on site or radio link your pictures and sound back to base.

If you are recording a concert, some of the camera positions may take up audience seating, so it may be necessary to compensate the venue for lost income.

There may also be restrictions on the number of places where the scanner can park or the precise positioning of the cameras and cables. For most events arrangements need to be made to hide camera cables. At some golfing events, for example, people will spend hours covering up cables with leaves, usually brought in specially for the occasion!

### Police permission

Is police permission necessary for parking the scanner? If you are recording material in the street you will certainly need help with crowd control and the police must be informed in case you cause traffic problems. They have every right to stop the recording if you end up inadvertently causing a breach of the peace.

### Restricted views for audience

If the OB is in a cathedral, for example, extra monitors may be provided for those members of the congregation with a restricted view of the proceedings.

### Safety

Scaffolding may need to be erected and a lot of safety factors taken into consideration. A stage manager will be present for rehearsals and recordings and he will be in charge of safety. Every effort should be made for the SM to be present at the planning meeting, in order to sort out safety factors as soon as possible. Larger organisations have safety specialists who can help.

### Anyone got another coin for the meter?

Whether you are using public or private property as a base for the scanner, you may be tapping into their electricity supply for power. This must be arranged in advance. Or you may take your own generator to remain self-sufficient, which will be yet another vehicle needing a parking space.

### Costume and make-up

You may need to arrange for rooms to be used for costume and make-up. Are there enough power sockets to plug in the necessary hairdryers and mirror lights? Is there running water, etc?

If costume and make-up caravans are to be used, make sure there will be enough space for the extra vehicles, with easy access to the recording area.

### Who moved the sun?

The position of the sun and how this will affect camera positions will have to be checked. There may be problems with daylight, so drapes may be required to mask off windows.

### Plan B

If the heavens open on the morning of the event check whether plan B exists. You may need to type a completely different script and camera cards in case it is implemented. So allow time.

### Technical requirements

By the end of the planning meeting your director will produce the technical requirements, covering everything necessary for the production. Add any extras which will help, such as contacts, telephone numbers, transport arrangements, etc. The technical requirements should be distributed to all those concerned with the OB, and they will form the groundwork for any future discussions on the production.

Apart from the technical aspects, there are many other things which will need to be considered, and should be attached to the technical requirements.

- Where will you all park? If not possible at the location you will need to arrange transport to the site.

- Do you need to hire caterers?

- Do you need to book accommodation for everyone?

- What are the travel arrangements?

- Will people need special passes to get on site?

- Who will supply accreditation?

Basically, organise everything you need to get yourself to the location for the duration of the production and then make similar arrangements for everyone else.

Check up on previous OBs of a similar nature — there will still be the technical requirements from that occasion to give you a point of reference.

### Advertising/sponsorship

This is a difficult matter which does need consideration. Take advice on what the situation is if you are in doubt, rather than have difficulties after the recording. There could be obvious problems when, for example, participants' T-shirts brandish the name of a sponsor.

### Accommodation

Booking accommodation for everyone can be a real headache, so arrange it as soon as possible. Take advantage of hotel discounts, but make sure they can accommodate strange eating times for large numbers, if applicable. If the OB is a drama production, you may need to arrange banking facilities to pay artists' expenses whilst away.

## Things to include in the technical requirements

**Staffing**: all the people connected with your production, including contacts at the venue, police where appropriate, and sponsors or co-ordinators of the event.

**Location**: full details, including maps and directions.

**Access**: details for entrance, and where passes can be collected. Accreditation would be one of your tasks in planning the production.

**Schedule**: details of schedule, day-by-day. Include rigging and de-rigging time. Give times of performances or transmission details where appropriate.

**Vision**: details of all camera positions, plus any moves as appropriate. (Golfing events will often have two or three positions for each camera).

**Sound**: details of all sound circuits required, ranging from commentary positions to production talkback circuits.

**In vision**: details for in-vision presentation position, including sound and vision circuits. (This position may well need set dressing).

**Graphics**: details of all graphics input into the production, either caption scanners, slides or caption generators.

**Production caravan**: details of location and equipment.

**Lighting**: full details of positions of lights and cabling.

**Communications**: sound and vision lines, production talkbacks, feeds to VT recording van or back to base.

**Catering**: details of all available catering, or details of what will be supplied.

## Remember the kitchen sink!

Take everything you will need — and more — with you when you leave base for your OB. There is no point in having a booking sheet or a vital telephone number back in the office. It is a nuisance to carry everything with you, but it is important that you do. Always take a spare of everything because, when you are away from base, it may not be too easy to get a replacement. Certainly a spare watch is essential, along with aspirins, first aid kit, etc, etc, etc (see p.152).

## Scripts and running orders

There may not be the opportunity before leaving base to produce a complete script, but some kind of running order should get you going, and may even act as the final script in some circumstances. Whatever state it is in have lots with you. Photocopiers are thin on the ground in the middle of a field!

In the case of State occasions, the event itself will dictate your coverage. Through careful pre-planning with the organisers, you will know the structure and timing of the procession.

Similarly in a golf tournament, the director will move between tee shots, fairways and the greens to cover the main players in the event. Spotters are out with the players keeping track of the scores which are passed on through you to the commentators.

In the case of an unrehearsed music concert or ice-skating event, you may have attended a rehearsal or performance with the director, taken notes and, during recording/transmission have to race read the event to make sure the cameramen cover the action adequately. (More details in Chapter 17).

## Camera cards

Check with the engineering manager or camera supervisor what sort of cameras they have and whether camera cards can be fitted to them. They are usually side-mounted for OB cameras and often quarter size.

So, if in doubt, punch holes on all sides and take a supply of tape and clips to cope with any situation. A rough guide for the numbers of cards required is:

| CAMERA | NUMBER OF CARDS |
|---|---|
| Lightweight | 1 set, half A4 size |
| Plover | 1 set |
| Kestrel | 2 sets |
| Tern | 1 set |
| Falcon | 2 sets |
| Nike | 3 or 4 sets |

### Portable typewriter

You may find you need to take a portable typewriter and do the script on site. This could be transported in the props van and stored in the production caravan. Or you may find your hotel room becomes the stand-by office.

### Graphics

Collect graphics early and check thoroughly. Once you are away from base it is going to be virtually impossible to make changes.

### The mobile production control room

The mobile production control room (or scanner) can be very tight for space, so there is rarely enough room on the desk in front of you to lay out the scripts as you would do in a normal studio. You just have to adapt to the space provided.

If you are involved in, say, a sporting event where you can't get out of the scanner for hours on end, do the sensible thing and avoid drinking too much tea before you start! You often find there isn't a toilet for miles and whilst the chaps are happy to nip off into the bushes, you may feel less inclined to do so. Better to be thirsty than bursting!

### Recordings on site and back at base

If you are recording the programme, it may be recorded on site or back at base. Remember to get spool numbers at the end of the day. Also find out how the tapes are going to get back to base, as they may be needed for editing early the next day and you may have to take them back yourself.

### Editec

There may also be a fast turn round to transmission, so you will need time code notes for editing. Alternatively, the programme may be compiled as you go along, in which case you may encounter editec.

This is a simple way of recording material in stages; for example, take a swimming event. Once one section is complete, VT will spin back ten seconds, and the director will stand everyone by. You then count down from fifteen and at ten VT will drop into record and the proceedings simply continue on cue.

In this way you can eliminate inessential pauses between events, etc. At the end of the recording, you will have a completed package ready for transmission.

The BBC only tend to use this method with sport, but other companies use it more widely.

### Live transmissions

If you are transmitting live into the network, make sure you can see a cue dot in order to get on air. If you are out of the main network region, a special feed of network to the scanner may be required so you can get on air correctly.

The engineering manager will have organised telephone communications which may mean using a standard 'phone for cueing your programme on air if no network feed is possible. There is more information about getting an OB "on air" in Chapter 11, *The Lightning Guide to Live Galleries.*

## Speedy location (film & OB) checklist

- Attend planning meeting

- Go on the recce if possible

- Find your contacts at the venue

- Seek police permission where appropriate

- Check power supplies and acoustics

- Type out technical requirements and distribute

- Type out film schedule and distribute

- Book accommodation early

- Arrange passes and accreditation early

- Arrange facilities payments and contracts

- Book post-production facilities early

- Arrange parking on site

- Book hospitality/catering

- Book and take graphics/audience tickets, etc

- Arrange banking facilities near site

- Order maps and plans of site and immediate location

- Contact numbers police/local doctors/dentists/ hospitals, etc.

## Thinks to take on location

- Scripts/running orders/recording orders
- Camera cards (check OB cameras for size and number)
- Technical requirements
- Programme file
- Contact numbers for all production/crew/contributors
- Notepads
- Writing implements
- Stopwatches
- Polaroid
- Spare stationery/staplers/bulldog clips/sellotape, etc.
- Logging sheets/shot list forms
- Tickets/passes/accreditation
- Typewriter if appropriate
- Paracetamol, etc.
- Spares of everything
- Correct clothing for the occasion (allow for wet/cold/hot)

## Foreign locations checklist

- Check permits/visas/passports
- Innoculations/medical requirements
- Money/insurance — local banking arrangements
- Travel carnet for equipment/excess baggage
- Check local customs
- Clothing restrictions
- Local helpers/interpreters
- Check for local events/national holidays, etc.
- Clapperboard
- Film stock

# Chapter 15

# Introduction to Magazine Programmes

# PART IV

The term 'magazine' programme encompasses a multitude of sins, from live current affairs programmes, through to carefully rehearsed recordings of childrens programmes, chat shows, quiz shows, etc. This chapter will aim to cover all the elements involved in this type of programme.

### Setting up a magazine programme

Setting up a magazine programme can often be easier than other types of programmes. Although the run may be longer, the programmes will tend to follow a set pattern. The problem is getting a system designed to suit the programme — once you are into the run you will not have time to re-think it.

### The budget

Magazine programmes tend to be strand programmes and will be given a strand budget which means your budget will be divided up into the number of programmes in the run, and you will either cost each weekly programme separately or, if you are working on a daily programme, you may well do a weekly budget covering five programmes.

### The production file

As with any type of programme, you will need to start up production files and keep track of anything connected with the programme. Depending on the type of programme, you can either start up one file for each weekly programme, or work on a weekly file to cover however many programmes you transmit per week.

### Planning meetings

Planning meetings for your programme might well be cut down to one main session before the start of the run. Everyone connected with the programme meets up to discuss all the continuous elements of the programme, such as setting and lighting. Then, on a weekly basis, you may get away with a mini-planning meeting or even 'phone calls to fine tune the master plan.

## Booking resources

A lot of the resources connected with the programme can be block booked through your resources department, so that the same facilities will turn up each week for however many weeks of the run.

It's a headache getting the first block bookings out of the way, but once that is done, it saves you the weekly task of bookings. It is, however, always advisable to check each week, that your usual bookings are all present and correct.

## Servicing departments

You may well find that certain service departments, such as make-up, will allocate someone on the day and will expect nothing unusual to occur in the programme. But do make sure if your presenter is, for example, expecting to have her hair washed and blow dried, that you have allowed enough time before rehearsals or recordings start.

Each week it is up to you, to find the names of all those contributing to your programme from service departments, so that everyone knows who is involved with the programme on any one day. This information can then go on the front page of the script.

## Graphics

The graphics input to a current affairs programme is often a very last-minute affair, whereas a planned magazine programme has the luxury of ordering graphics in advance.

Until very recently graphics tended to be 'hard' graphics, that is, captions stuck on caption card and placed on caption stands in the studio with a camera pointing at them, or 35mm slides. Nowadays, the graphics revolution has turned all that into electronic wizardry. Pictures are created and stored on floppy discs and electronic slide files. They allow flexibility with last-minute changes, but also cause problems with their complexity. It is an escalating phenomenon which changes and develops daily. It is also an extremely expensive facility. Keep up to date!

### Name superimpositions

As part of the graphics revolution name superimpositions have altered dramatically in the last few years. They can be created in a variety of styles on a variety of machines. Aston, Chyron, Ryley are a number of the trade names for the machines that produce the modern name 'supers'.

Put simply, they are a sophisticated typewriter connected to a floppy disk, where information can be stored and recalled in any order. Many smaller production companies require the PA to operate these as well as do the timings, so it is a skill worth learning.

### Programme inserts

Quite often there isn't enough time (or money) to send a PA on the filming trips for inserts into the programme, which often creates more problems than it solves. Remember always, therefore, to check on all the material going into the inserts, from artists payments, to music copyright, etc.

If you do go filming, it is very likely to be on the one day of the week you could have had off within the studio schedule!

Different programmes have different methods of costing insert material. It isn't always certain at the time of filming which programme an insert will be used in, so separate insert costing numbers can be created to identify costs once a programme schedule has been arranged. You can then just add everything under your insert number to the main costs of each programme.

### Keeping up to date

Once into a run of programmes, you will soon find the snowball effect taking over. It is essential to keep up to date with everything and clear one programme out of the way before the next one descends upon you.

It can be a gruelling time working on a strand or long-running series. Don't fall into the trap of thinking the paperwork will take care of itself. It won't. You must pace the production and work out a checklist on how to get through the week, giving yourself enough time to wrap up one programme and prepare for the next.

There are mixed feelings about PAs working on the location shoots of a magazine programme, as they are comparatively straightforward in terms of content, containing mainly factual information and interviews where the director takes his own shot list.

If you are the only PA on a daily production, there clearly isn't enough time in the schedule for you to go on location and you will simply be given all the information ready for the studio part of the programme, such as timings and 'in' and 'out' cues. So, such a tight schedule means you have missed what might have been a welcome break from the office/studio routine.

On the other hand, if there is more than one PA and you are alternating the studio part of the programme, you should be able to fit at least one location day into your schedule, as well as having enough time to complete the paperwork.

It also means that if a PA is on location, you reduce the chances of any problems with post-production paperwork or contractual requirements.

**News programmes**

The PA's role will vary with news programmes. The emphasis is very much on the gallery work and there is far less paperwork to deal with, but you could be involved in four or five bulletins a day. The editorial team for news may be divided into the relevant programmes and you move around to each team as the day progresses.

You are likely only to be involved with the PasC either for the programmes you did or on a shift which brings you in for a paperwork day.

### Suggested checklist for magazine type programme

Using the example of a programme recorded in the studio on a Thursday, for Saturday transmission, block book your main facilities at the start of the run.

MONDAY
Wrap up costing
Thank you letters
Attend planning meeting
PasC

TUESDAY
Book facilities for next programme — dressing rooms, extra insert machines, etc
Book graphics
Book artists and contributors
Start outline of script where possible (front page, etc)

WEDNESDAY
Type camera script and camera cards
Check all facilities (final details of machines, etc.)

THURSDAY
Studio — all day
Distribute scripts to all necessary places
Clip camera cards to camera
Check dressing rooms with reception
Inform security of all contributors and guests

FRIDAY
Attend editing session
Time final programme duration
Prepare transmission details — and take to presentation
Inform duty office of any information in programme

SATURDAY AND SUNDAY
Days off — but don't count on it. There could be filming to do or just so much work that, during the run you need to come in one day over the weekend.

# Chapter 16

# Drama   Productions

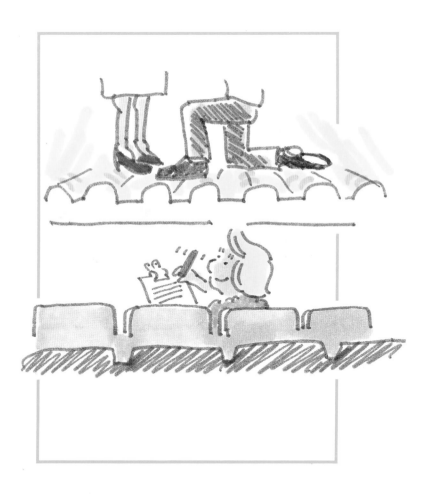

On a drama production the PA usually works within an immediate team of four people — the director, production manager and assistant floor manager. There will probably be several such teams working on a strand/series/serial under the overall control of a producer.

Working with the producer will be a script editor and a production associate. In order to put the PA's role into perspective I have set out below a brief description of each of the team members' jobs.

### Producer

The producer will have overall control of all aspects of the programme or strand of programmes for which he is responsible.

### Production associate

The production associate assists the producer in the translation of scripts into costed facilities, in the preparation of budgets and in the financial and logistical control of a programme or strand. He advises on locations and facilities required and maintains liaison between production teams.

### Script editor

The role of the script editor varies in practice according to the type of programme in which he is working. However, it is fundamental to ensure that scripts commissioned by producers are of the highest standard, are in accordance with the producer's brief and are in a usable form for production at the time required. Once a script has been accepted, the script editor becomes the author's representative — with particular regard to the observance of contractual obligations.

### Director

The director is the 'leader' of the team in which the PA works, and is responsible for the technical and artistic realisation of the script in all its aspects. As the PA on a drama, you will work most closely with the director.

### Production assistant

The production assistant works to the director and is responsible for the administrative work required before, during and after the production. She looks after continuity on location and acts as the director's immediate assistant in the studio gallery.

### Production manager

As the senior member of the director's team, the PM is responsible to him for putting into operation the production requirements during the preparation, filming, rehearsal and recording of the programme. The PM is also responsible for the safety of staff and artists both on location and in the studio.

### Assistant floor manager

The AFM, in association with the designer, is responsible to the director and PM for ordering, selecting, setting and safe-keeping of action props for rehearsal, on location and in the studio. The AFM marks up the rehearsal room floor and, during rehearsals, keeps an accurate script noting artists' moves and all changes in dialogue which he will pass on to the PA. The AFM will often assist with the continuity of action props on location and in the studio.

## SETTING UP A DRAMA PROGRAMME

As with most productions, the first thing to do is to set up the office the way you like it and to ensure that you have all the necessary forms and stationery required during the production. Drama seems to generate far more paperwork than other programmes, so do get organised early.

Now is the time to make up your wall charts: one with useful contact numbers and another with your casting requirements. An at-a-glance breakdown of cast movements will prove invaluable.

Make sure you don't put any confidential contact numbers on wall charts which could be copied by passers by. You may also want to mark up a calendar with such things as filming dates, rehearsals, editing and dubbing dates, etc.

Whilst everything is still relatively quiet you should read through the scripts to get the feel of the story and to familiarise yourself with the characters and plot.

### Negative checks

Neg checks need to be carried out on any information contained in a script which may cause embarrassment on transmission; it could be the use of an address or telephone number which is seen or quoted in the programme. For example, where possible, make sure the audience don't actually see any addresses on letters or postcards or a clear shot of a telephone number. It can cause tremendous problems for the real owners of those addresses and telephone numbers.

### Timings

It is important to time the scenes as you read through the script — the director and script editor will also do this; sometimes you all take parts and time a read through. If the programme is under or over length, the script editor should be advised and dialogue or scenes can be added or dropped as required.

### Rehearsal scripts

Once a version of the script has been agreed for rehearsals, print up enough to keep things going. When sending them out to potential artists you should print at the top of the front page the following phrase which is self-explanatory: "The sending of this script does not constitute the offer of a contract for any part in it".

### The story order

You may find that someone has already done a story order for you, but if there isn't one available, get together with the production manager and work one out. Basically the story order is a *précis* of each scene, including the characters, locations and time of day. As you do the story order try to be aware of direct and indirect continuity between scenes.

## Costume and make-up requirements

At this stage think about what costume and make-up requirements you have. List the characters and make notes against them as you go through the script, then talk to the director.

Consolidate your ideas and send off a costume and make-up plot to your designers. Get in touch with the costume designer and make-up artist and arrange for them to meet the director (the PM should be present at this meeting).

## Casting

It is quite likely that you will, in some way, be involved in the casting process — this is where you will need copies of *Spotlight* and *Contacts*. The director usually has some idea of who he sees as a particular character or he may look through *Spotlight* and choose several artists. When this has been done, you can check the artists' availability with their agents and arrange a convenient time and place for an audition. If you are working on a large production you may have the luxury of a casting director who will select artists and arrange auditions.

As mentioned on p.47, NEVER discuss money with agents or artists. Just call for 'an availability check' and say no more — the rest will be done by your artist booker.

## Auditions

You may be required to set up auditions for the director. Check where he wants to hold them, find a suitably large office and preferably a comfortable room for people to wait in.

When the director has decided who he wants, pass the details on to your artist booker who will offer the part and negotiate the fee.

Once agreed, you can follow this up with a confirmation letter and any details he may need to know. Once a booking is confirmed, obtain the artist's home address and telephone number from the agent and send out a script. You should also inform costume and make-up.

### General notes on booking artists

Try to speak to the artist booker as early as possible and send him a requisition form with the characters listed on it even if you don't know which artists you want — he will fill in the name and the agent's details when the booking has been made.

You should send your booker a script as soon as possible so that he can assess the 'weight' and contribution of each part.

Be sure to let the booker know all the dates you require the artist for — even if they are months apart, as it makes a difference to the fee paid.

### Supporting artists and walk-ons

Supporting artists are the performers who are not required to give individual characterisations or to speak even a word of scripted dialogue, except as crowd noises.

A walk-on can utter a few more words, but is still unscripted and receives no individual direction.

### Special skills

Check to see if there are any special requirements for the part, e.g. ability to drive, hair cuts, lots of costume fitting, danger or nudity! All of these will affect the contract.

### Children

If you have children (under age sixteen) in your programme, make sure you get them cast early so that a licence can be arranged. Speak to the booker who will advise on the details. The local authority will need to be sent forms well in advance and arrangements must be made for chaperones, as well as tutoring if filming is during school time.

There are strict rules and regulations governing the hours under sixteens may work, details of which are outlined in Chapter 7 under *Contracts*. This must be followed religiously and local authority inspectors can call on the production at any time to check up. So keep the licencing details with you and adhere to the rules.

Whilst you are busy sorting out all the above, the PM will be on a location recce and the AFM will be making prop lists. Let us assume you are fully cast, the artists' photos are on the wall, and your chart is filled in.

## The location recce

The PM has taken the director, cameraman, lighting gaffer and designer to see the film locations. If you can go too, so much the better, but usually there isn't time.

## Location arrangements

When locations have been agreed, the PM will arrange location facility contracts and accommodation for everyone going on the shoot. Of course, it is likely to fall to the PA to make the actual hotel bookings, so liaise with the PM and find out how much he can do and what you need to organise.

The PM should give you the film schedule complete with all the details — allow plenty of time to type a schedule as they are always weighty documents. Be sure to have it printed and distributed at least one week prior to filming in case there are problems and queries which can then be ironed out before leaving base.

## Shooting script

If you are very lucky, the director will give you a shooting script or shot list before you go filming. This can be useful as a guideline for what he intends to shoot, but will not be final.

# OFF ON LOCATION

You will need to take quite a lot on location. Some of the bulkier items such as typewriter, spare scripts, schedules, etc could go on the props van or with the AFM. Some of the other things you will need are suggested below:

Continuity sheets
Spare story orders
Spare location script
Scenes (in story order)
Polaroid camera and film
Letterhead paper and envelopes
Large envelopes (addressed to film editor)
Stopwatches (and a spare, if possible)
Lined paper
Cast address list
Useful numbers (contacts) list
Child licences
Artists' time sheets
Snap outs
Programme file(s)
Contracts
Note pads
Pens, pencils, erasers, rulers, etc.

Don't forget a cash advance to cover all your costs whilst away from base. You may well be dealing with artists' expenses as well. If extra large amounts of money are involved, you can make arrangements for drawing out cash at a local bank.

**Who says what**

For those new to film there is a routine of who says what on location, which will be found in Chapter 13 on p.126.

**Continuity**

Once on location, your main job is the continuity — don't let yourself be distracted from that job, either by other people asking you to do something such as keeping on-lookers quiet or by being sent off to check out the next location. Your head will be on the block if the continuity goes wrong, so shut everything else out and concentrate!

The subject of continuity is very complicated and it will take a long time for you to discover the best method of taking notes so that you feel relaxed and confident about them. It would take another whole book to go into the precise art of continuity*, so this chapter will cover the subject superficially.

It is important for you to familiarise yourself fully with the script before you get out on location and you will find that the story order is a useful quick reference document which you can use to highlight areas of direct and indirect continuity.

As well as the story order, you should always carry a full script in story order with you.

Try to find out how the director intends to cover a scene. This will help you to form a mental picture of the shots and how they are cut together. Remember continuity only exists within a scene after the first angle has been shot, so try to work things out from angle-to-angle and shot-to-shot. If you know where the important junctions for cuts will be, you can pay particular attention to the continuity at those points.

It is fairly safe to assume that the first shot of a scene will be the master or establishing shot, and the rest of the coverage will follow, (2-shots, singles, cutaways, etc).

Continuity is not just a question of being good at observation — but of knowing *what* to observe. **Direct continuity** means that actions are carried over from one scene to the next with no time lapses. **Indirect continuity** refers to links between scenes that are not consecutive.

Firstly, establish what the shot size is — easy if you have a monitor; if you are unsure, either check with the director or ask the cameraman if you can have a look through the lens.

*See *Continuity Notes*, Roger Singleton-Turner and Gill Partridge, BBC Television Training

Here are some pointers for continuity with different shot sizes:

CU (close up)— pay particular attention to eyelines. Worry about props if they come into frame (i.e. cigarettes, drinks, etc). Don't worry about the artist's whole costume, but concentrate on collars, ties, scarves, etc. Also keep an eye on hair.

MS (mid-shot) — try to be aware of the whole shot!

WS (wide shot)— don't attempt to note down every detail or prop and action, but try to see the whole scene and think about where you are cutting into it. Think about the extras crossing frame, etc and, of course, the main characters' actions.

LS (long shot)— you need not worry about small details but watch the action, as you may well cut straight in on it. E.g. cars driving up, people getting out and so on.

An accurate shot description is essential for your notes and to match continuity from shot-to-shot and scene-to-scene. Always note where the shot begins and ends, both in terms of dialogue and action.

Note the way your artists enter and leave frame — do so from your viewpoint, which is also that of the camera. E.g. Anne enters R/f and exits L/f. Know the correct terminology and be consistent in your use of it.

If it helps, draw diagrams for your rough notes, noting artists' movements — they may help later on when matching shots and eyelines.

As a general rule your set designer will be in charge of set dressing and your AFM will be in charge of action props. They will both keep an eye on the props but, as you can't rely on them to do so, make a note of the general position of relevant props (either by diagram or polaroid). Pay particular attention to action props and where they are used in relation to dialogue.

It is generally true to say that the more that is happening in a shot, the less continuity matters. However, in a 1+1 situation every move matters — for example, where an actor is drinking a glass of wine, eating and holding a conversation.

Watch the camera rehearsals closely — the artists will be setting their moves in their own minds and will hopefully follow them in the actual take. Keep all your early jottings in light pencil for later reference.

At this point you can write up the basic shot description on your continuity note pad, be it master 2-shot, single or whatever. Never rely on your memory, but put everything down which will help you. You can always leave off your little scribbles and diagrams when you write the notes up neatly for the editor.

On the master shot, note down action in relation to dialogue and then, when you come to the cut in shot, you can check that the artists repeat what they did in the master. Let the director, know if they do not, you may then go for a retake or the director might say "That doesn't matter, I won't be using that bit" — always make a note on your editing sheets of such remarks to save your own skin when questions are asked later.

At the same time, mark up your script with tramlines showing the start and finish of all shots. The editor can then see at a glance how shots can fit with the dialogue and action.

### When and where to type up your continuity notes

Some PAs type up their continuity notes between scenes, whilst still on location, others leave it to the end of the day when they can mark up a coverage script as well. Both the continuity notes and the coverage script will be sent off with the rushes and passed on to the film editor. Examples of a marked up script with tramlines from location and the matching continuity sheet are on pp.170 and 171 respectively.

### Polaroid cameras

Make sure you have one at the top of your packing list; they help enormously on a long, complicated shoot. They can also help ease one of a PA's biggest headaches — continuity on

# Specimen: Drama Script with Tramlines from Location

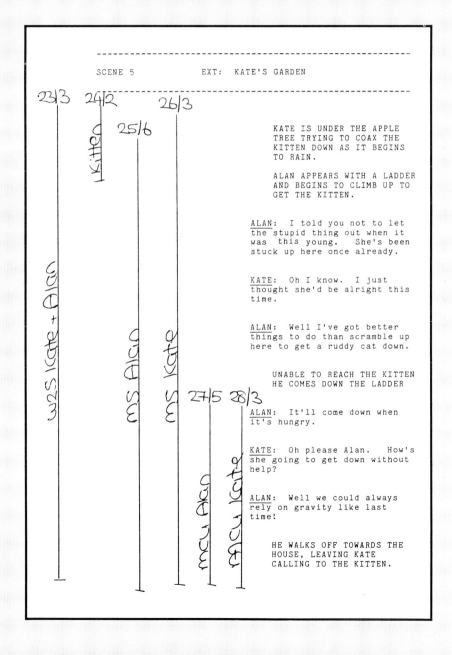

----------------------------------------------------------------

SCENE 5                EXT:   KATE'S GARDEN

----------------------------------------------------------------

23/3    24/2        26/3

25/6

Kitten

KATE IS UNDER THE APPLE
TREE TRYING TO COAX THE
KITTEN DOWN AS IT BEGINS
TO RAIN.

ALAN APPEARS WITH A LADDER
AND BEGINS TO CLIMB UP TO
GET THE KITTEN.

ALAN:  I told you not to let
the stupid thing out when it
was  this young.   She's been
stuck up here once already.

KATE:  Oh I know.  I just
thought she'd be alright this
time.

ALAN:  Well I've got better
things to do than scramble up
here to get a ruddy cat down.

UNABLE TO REACH THE KITTEN
HE COMES DOWN THE LADDER

27/5  28/3

ALAN:  It'll come down when
it's hungry.

KATE:  Oh please Alan.  How's
she going to get down without
help?

ALAN:  Well we could always
rely on gravity like last
time!

HE WALKS OFF TOWARDS THE
HOUSE, LEAVING KATE
CALLING TO THE KITTEN.

32S Kate + Alan

ES Alan

ES Kate

MCU Alan

MCU Kate

# Specimen: Drama Continuity Sheet

**BBC TV FILM CONTINUITY NOTES**   Date: 17/9/9C

| Programme | Kate + Alan | Episode no. or sub title | | Slate no. 23 |
|---|---|---|---|---|
| Costing no. | | | | |

| Set-up/location | | Int. | Day | Sync / Silent | Sequence no. |
|---|---|---|---|---|---|
| Kate's Garden | | Ext. | Night | Guidetrack with camera | Shot no. |
| | | Script page no. 22 | | Shot list page no. | |

Costume/make-up/prop notes

| Sound Roll No. | 3 | | | | | | | |
|---|---|---|---|---|---|---|---|---|
| Film Roll No. | 5 | | | | | | | |
| circle TAKES printed | 1 | 2 | ③ | 4 | 5 | 6 | 7 | 8 |
| End board | | | | | | | | |
| TIMING | 42" | 44" | 41" | | | | | |
| FOOTAGE | | | | | | | | |
| REASON for use or n/g | NG - fluff | NG - over- lapping dialogue | Gd. | | | | | |

**SHOT DESCRIPTION**

WS. Kate by apple tree Alan enters L and exits L.

**DIALOGUE**

Alan: I told you not to let . . .

Alan . . . gravity like last time

ANY WILD TRACK/S RECORDED AFTER THIS SLATE

PS/507 1.87

block filming for a series. They also help back at base for checking continuity between location and studio scenes.

### Rushes viewing

If you are away on location for a long shoot, you could arrange for a VHS copy of the sync rushes to be sent back to you on location, but don't forget, you might also have to arrange for a monitor and VHS player to view the rushes at your hotel.

### Back home after filming

Get your paperwork up to date — artists' time sheets filled in, expenses claimed, thank you letters done, etc. At the same time you may have additional casting going on for the studio scenes.

### Timing of location inserts

Get timings from the film editor when inserts are complete and get a VHS copy made for your office use. Then time the scenes again with the director (there may be some 'early outs' that you should note), but make sure this does not affect the continuity between scenes.

### Continuity between location inserts and studio

It is also useful to check continuity of costume and action at this time and make sure that the master script is up-dated with any dialogue changes arising from the filming.

## POST FILMING AND PRE-STUDIO

### The read through

This may well be the first time the full cast have met. Your AFM will arrange the rehearsal room for the read through. It is also a time when costume and make-up can arrange costume and wig fittings.

## Rehearsals

The AFM will have taken the floor plan and marked up the rehearsal room floor and arranged rehearsal props. He will attend all rehearsals and mark up a script as the scenes are blocked, communicating all dialogue changes to you daily.

The AFM will also keep a check on scene timings and the programme running time (including titles and location scenes) and will advise the script editor if there are any problems. If anyone extra has been cast for the studio, advise costume and make-up.

If time allows, attend at least some rehearsals so you become familiar with the feel and pace of the programme.

## Planning meetings/technical runs

In liaison with the director and the PM, you should arrange a planning meeting/technical run and producer's run with design, costume, make-up, props, lighting director, technical co-ordinator, sound supervisor, senior cameraman, production team, producer, script editor and production associate.

## Recording order

The PM will have worked out a recording order for the studio day and given it to you for typing — check through it to make sure it works. If you have any doubts, speak to the PM, then get him to check it before printing.

Print it as early as possible, and send it to costume and make-up. Once they have agreed it, it should be distributed to all those attending the planning meeting.

## Graphics

If you have any graphics to order, do so promptly, but check all details with the producer before requisitioning them. Alterations can be time wasting and costly and much will depend on the format of your graphics.

# Specimen: Drama Recording Order

```
==================================================================
PAGE    SCENE/SET    D/N        CAST         CAMS/BOOMS   SHOTS
==================================================================

15  3. OFFICE     DAY 1      GERALD       1A 2A 3B     29-36
                  0930       PETER
                             CAROL
                             MARY
------------------------------------------------------------------
/ / / / / / / /    R E C O R D I N G   P A U S E  / / / / / /
------------------------------------------------------------------


18     4. CANTEEN  DAY 1      GERALD       2B 3C 4A     37-42
                   1230       PETER
                              HAROLD
------------------------------------------------------------------
/ / / / / / / /    R E C O R D I N G   P A U S E  / / / / / /
------------------------------------------------------------------

21     5. RECEPTION DAY 2     HENRY        1A 2B 3B     44-48
                    0800      PETER

==================================================================
               R E C O R D I N G    B R E A K

    TK 1 - OPENING TITLES  (0.35")
    TK 2 - KATE'S GARDEN   (0.56")

    Peter costume change (wet rain coat)
==================================================================

25    15. RECEPTION DAY 2     PETER        2A           84
                    1730

------------------------------------------------------------------
/ / / / / / / /    R E C O R D I N G   P A U S E  / / / / / /
------------------------------------------------------------------


23     6. LOUNGE   DAY 2      ANNE         1A 3A 4B     49-55
                   1945       ROSS

------------------------------------------------------------------
/ / / / / / / /    R E C O R D I N G   P A U S E  / / / / / /
------------------------------------------------------------------


24     7. BEDROOM  DAY 2      ANNE         2A           56
                   2000

------------------------------------------------------------------
/ / / / / / / /    R E C O R D I N G   P A U S E  / / / / / /
------------------------------------------------------------------
```

## Getting ahead

- Do the front page of the camera script (see p.96).
- Book extras/walk-ons, in liaison with PM.
- Book dressing rooms.
- Attend tech/prod runs and take plenty of spare recording orders. Time the scenes as you run through and make sure you calculate the total running time at the end of each run (somebody is bound to ask for it!)

If there are no technical problems and costume, make-up and design are happy, then the recording order can remain as it is and you can breathe a sigh of relief!

## The camera script

The director will now mark up his script with camera shots and, via the PM, pass the script on to you for typing. He will mark up the cameras on the floor plan and check that the camera positions on the script work. Then the PM will mark up a clear copy of the floor plan so that lighting and sound can finalise their plots for the studio. You, in the meantime, begin the mammoth task of typing up the shots on to the final script.

You may well find that one scene contains many shots and to squeeze them all on to the existing text would confuse people. You should, therefore, adjust the layout of the script to allow for the numbers of shots.

As I mention in Chapter 12, (and it is never more true than with drama scripts) — never try to save money by saving paper. A bunched-up text with lots of shots on it will only waste time in the gallery during rehearsal as no one can decipher it easily. If you have any queries about the script, speak to either the PM or director.

If you have time, do your camera cards before you get the bulk of the scripts printed (you usually spot mistakes when you are doing the cards). If you don't have time, run off one copy and work from that whilst the rest of the scripts are being printed. Set aside a lot of time for the script and the camera cards —

many a PA in drama burns the midnight oil at this stage of the production. Refer to Chapter 12 for script and camera card layouts, which has examples of drama scripts on pp.105 and 106.

The script will need to be assembled in recording order for the studio and the pages should be re-numbered in ink so everyone knows where they are. It is still advisable, however, to keep a rough copy of the script with you in story order for any queries.

Once the scripts are back from printing, mark up the essential ones with all the changes you know.

# THE STUDIO DAY

### Before rehearsals start

Get in early on the studio recording day, as there is a lot to do before the rehearsals start. Distribute scripts to all who need one. Take camera cards and running orders on to the studio floor, and try to find the senior cameraman, otherwise fix the cards on to the appropriate cameras.

Leave a number of scripts on the floor, but not too many. Make sure all other contributing sources to your studio have scripts, such as VT recording machines, VT/TK play-in machines, reception, etc.

Distribution of scripts to certain places can be done by post or delivered the day before, but some of them have a daily clear out of scripts, so it is safer to do the full tour on the recording day.

### During rehearsal/recording

In the gallery, it is your job to call shots, watch the continuity, keep a check on the dialogue, run in TK/VT inserts if required,

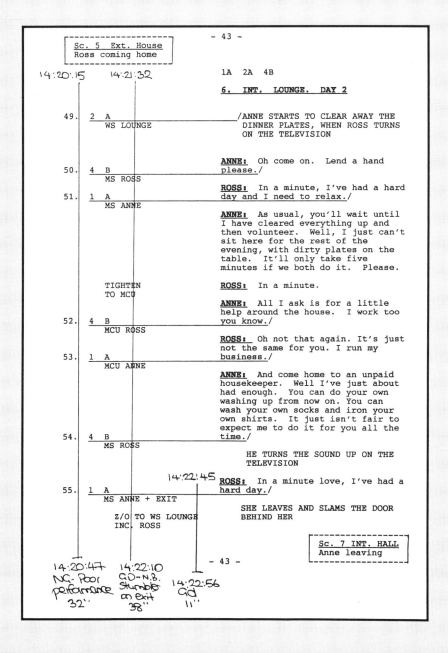

```
Sc. 5  Ext. House          - 43 -
Ross coming home

14:20:15    14:21:32        1A  2A  4B

                           6.  INT.  LOUNGE.  DAY 2

   49.  2  A                /ANNE STARTS TO CLEAR AWAY THE
          WS LOUNGE          DINNER PLATES, WHEN ROSS TURNS
                             ON THE TELEVISION

   50.  4  B                ANNE:  Oh come on.  Lend a hand
          MS ROSS           please./

   51.  1  A                ROSS:  In a minute, I've had a hard
          MS ANNE           day and I need to relax./

                           ANNE:  As usual, you'll wait until
                           I have cleared everything up and
                           then volunteer.  Well, I just can't
                           sit here for the rest of the
                           evening, with dirty plates on the
                           table.  It'll only take five
                           minutes if we both do it.  Please.

       TIGHTEN             ROSS:  In a minute.
       TO MCU
                           ANNE:  All I ask is for a little
                           help around the house.  I work too
   52.  4  B                you know./
          MCU ROSS
                           ROSS:  Oh not that again. It's just
                           not the same for you. I run my
   53.  1  A                business./
          MCU ANNE
                           ANNE:  And come home to an unpaid
                           housekeeper.  Well I've just about
                           had enough.  You can do your own
                           washing up from now on. You can
                           wash your own socks and iron your
                           own shirts.  It just isn't fair to
                           expect me to do it for you all the
   54.  4  B                time./
          MS ROSS
                           HE TURNS THE SOUND UP ON THE
                           TELEVISION

              14:22:45     ROSS:  In a minute love, I've had a
   55.  1  A               hard day./
          MS ANNE + EXIT
                           SHE LEAVES AND SLAMS THE DOOR
       Z/O TO WS LOUNGE    BEHIND HER
       INC. ROSS
                                   Sc. 7 INT. HALL
                                   Anne leaving

                           - 43 -

14:20:47   14:22:10   14:22:56
NG- Poor   GD-N.B.    Gd
performance Stumbles   11"
32"        on exit
           38"
```

log time code, keep an accurate time chart, do editing notes and director's notes. A detailed outline is covered in *The PAs Role in the Gallery* in Chapter 9.

## After the recording

Before leaving the gallery, do make sure that you have a note of VT spool numbers. Take all your notes and scribbles with you, as they will be needed for the editing session.

## Editing notes

Re-write or type out your time code editing notes (see below) as the director will want to take a VHS copy of the recording and your marked-up editing notes to prepare for the off-line edit.

| SPOOL NO | SC/TK | DESCRIPTION | TC IN | TC OUT | DUR |
|---|---|---|---|---|---|
| H106711 | TK 1 | Opening Titles | 14:10:00 | 14:10:35 | 0'35" |
| | Sc 1 | Shots 1 - 8 | 14:03:20 | 14:04:15 | 0' 5" |
| | Sc 2 | Shots 9 - 28 | 14:05:00 | 14:06:12 | 1'12" |
| | | P/up shot 25 | 14:07:00 | 14:07:30 | 0'30" |
| | Sc 3 | Shots 29 - 36 Tighten shot 30 | 14:07:53 | 14:08:30 | 0'37" |
| | Sc 4 | Shots 37 - 42 | 14:08:50 | 14:09:15 | 0'25" |
| | TK 2 | Kate's Garden | 14:10:55 | 14:11:51 | 0'56" |
| | Sc 5 | Shots 43 - 48 | 14:13:40 | 14:14:10 | 0'30" |
| | Sc 6 | Shots 49 - 55 | 14:21:32 | 14:22:10 | 0'38" |
| | | P/up shot 55 | 14:22:45 | 14:22:56 | 0'11" |
| | Sc 7 | Shot 56 | 14:23:12 | 14:23:28 | 0'16" |

### Off-line editing session

For larger drama productions, you may well find the producer/director wants to off-line the programme before the final edit. This is a cheaper way of checking edits on VHS — it is the video version of a film rough cut and allows for changes prior to the final master edit.

Remember, unlike film where you can insert extra shots after reviewing a cut copy, on VT you have to start with frame one and build up the programme shot-by-shot. You will need all your time code notes for this session and you will be able to double-check an overall programme duration.

### Editing and sypher dub

In the edit you can keep an eye on the running time and mark up the script with any additional dialogue changes. Once you have done the picture edit, you can get on with the sypher dub, details of which appear on p.53 in Chapter 8 on *The PA's Role in Post Production.*

### After the edit

After the edit and sypher, you are on the home stretch, but don't relax too soon! Drama productions above all others seem to generate the most post-production paperwork. For example, you will have a long script to bring up to date with all the changes, as an accurate copy of the transmitted programme.

There are likely to be publicity shots and copy required for specialist TV magazines and later for daily newspapers.

There will be a mountain of thank you letters and artists requiring notification of transmission date. Further details are mentioned in Chapter 8, *The PA's Role in Post Production.*

Once all that is over, it only remains for you to clear up the office, take all the charts off the walls and move on to your next production!

## Speedy checklist

- Set up production file
- Mark up wall wall charts
- Time the script
- Check for problems — neg checks
- Check locations with PM
- Artists availability
- Casting
- Artist bookings
- Costume and make-up requirements
- Book facilities
- Childrens' licences
- Location — take the kitchen sink
- Continuity
- Rushes viewings
- Planning meetings
- Script and camera cards
- Rehearsal/technical run
- Studio recording
- Off-line editing session
- Sypher
- Post production paperwork
- Transmission details
- Publicity photos, etc.
- Thank you letters

# Chapter 17

# Working with Music

You are bound to have some kind of music content in all but a handful of programmes. You might even find yourself working on a full-length music programme.

Apart from a music performance, there are other types of music that might occur in television such as incidental/background music or dramatico-musical works. Every programme will, at least, have an opening title sequence with music.

You can't escape it. If you are working on programmes, you are going to come across music in some form or other.

### Incidental or background music

Incidental or background music is when it is added to the programme to create more atmosphere or dramatic effect. The audience can hear the music but those appearing in the programme cannot.

### Visual music

Visual music is not only the obvious interpretation, where you can see someone playing an instrument or singing a song, but is also music from a radio in the room or the tune the window cleaner is whistling outside the window. It is music which the actors can hear. It might not be played in at the time of recording for ease of editing, but laid on later, for instance, juke box music in a pub scene. However, the artist might still be expected to react to it.

### Dramatico-musical

If the music involves acting or movement for the performers, this is known as dramatico-musical works, for example, opera or ballet.

### Contracts and copyright

Contracts and music reporting details are extremely complicated and an outline appears in the appropriate chapters, but you should always check with an expert before doing anything.

## Large music productions

This chapter will concentrate mainly on productions where music plays a large part, either in the form of a concert or as part of a ballet or opera.

## Preparation

The first thing you need to do is to find out what music is being used and order copies of it, either as scores, copies or lyrics, or even symbols on a page.

Do your research and find records, tapes or any recording of the music so that you know what to expect. You need to be totally familiar with it if you are going to do a professional and thorough job.

Start listening as far in advance of the recording or transmission of your programme as possible. If you are able to read music, then follow the score as you listen, so that you notice the difficult and fast passages.

The more familiar you are with the music in your programme, the more confident you will feel during the recording or transmission, and the more help you will be to the production. The nearer you get to the production date, the less time you will have to practise.

## Classical pieces

Sometimes special copies have to be obtained or made up and this can take two or three weeks. Find out the music and the edition to be used and order scores as soon as possible.

You will need copies for the director, vision mixer, sound supervisor, presenter and yourself. Have a couple of spare copies too. Ask the director and vision mixer what size of score they would like on the day. Mini-size scores which are about A5 are useful for practising with the music for reference, but they are rather small to use for scripting, and you will need two or three A4 size or larger scores for marking up.

## Specimen: Marked-Up Music Score

## Choosing the right size of score for easy working

Bear in mind that you may be in an OB scanner, where there isn't a lot of room. When ordering the music, ask if the repeats are written out in full. It is hard to follow a score in a studio situation if everyone has to keep flipping pages to and fro — it makes marking up difficult too.

Check also, that you can write direct on to the scores that have been sent. By the time you have finished with it, a score will be covered with figures, symbols and erasures.

## Marking up your score

Once the director has scripted the music, you will be given his copy of the score. If you are going to follow the score in the studio, you can mark up your copy from this in such a way that you will be able to follow it easily. Sometimes you may be sharing the score with the director, so ask if you can mark things more clearly if necessary.

As with a conventional dialogue script, you will need to number your shots. Write in the next camera before you turn the page, mark which camera you are on after a page turn and anything else which will help you keep your place.

Use a high-lighter pen to mark the distinctive pages of a theme in the music so that you will recognise them, such as a particularly loud retort from the trombone or a rumble from the timpani. The more signposts you can put in the better, but don't make the score so crowded that you are unable to find anything.

On the score you will see double dash marks which separate the systems (a group of staves) on the page. Make this clearer by ruling a red line across the page, so that you don't turn the page too soon. Tabs marking each movement in the score help you to turn to the right page quickly during rehearsals and, if there is a list of shot numbers included in each movement, it helps you to tell the cameraman quickly where the musicians are starting from before you've found the page yourself.

# Specimen: Grid System Script

CAMERA SCRIPT  NIELSEN FLUTE CONCERTO  SCORE PAGE 33

| SHOT | CAM 1 | CAM 2 | CAM 3 | CAM 4 | CAM 5 | NOTES ASTON |
|------|-------|-------|-------|-------|-------|-------------|
| 36 | | | | | MCU GALWAY | |
| 37 | | | | COND. & GALWAY & FRONT DESK STRINGS | | |
| 38 | | SLOW MIX MCU GALWAY DEVELOP | | | | |
| 39 | SLOW MIX W/A ORCH. & HALL | | | | | SUPER ALLEGRETTO |
| 40 | | | | MS COND. | | |

SHOT 41  CAM 3  NEXT

Above the staves you will often see a number or a letter: this is a method that the musician uses for finding a place in the score. Highlight these too, and when the conductor says "going from figure D", or "going from bar 90", you will also be able to find the place quickly and give the relevant shot number. Rehearsals with a conductor can move very quickly and you need to be alert and keep everyone informed as to what is happening.

**The grid system**

If you are unable to read music, take the director's marked-up score and pick out all the shot numbers and cameras and reformulate them in a grid or a plot.

From the example shown opposite, you will see that the cameras are listed across the top of the pages and the shot numbers down the side. You then fill in the corresponding square with the shot description.

Even if you are going to follow the score for the recording or transmission, it is a good idea to make up a grid. It helps when typing camera cards, and other people, such as lighting technicians and vision control, find it useful.

By looking at the grid, they can see at a glance which camera and shot is coming up and make any necessary adjustments to picture quality in advance. By following the grid, you can shot call in the usual way and preview the cameras thoroughly without getting confused by the complexity of a full score.

The disadvantage is that if some of the shots are not taken as planned, you can get lost. However, the vision mixer should call out which shot is going to be taken next. If you do get lost, just keep quiet until you can pick up again.

**Orchestras**

It can be useful to mark up the layout of an orchestra for the director, vision mixer and yourself, as well as for the cameramen.

# Specimen: Orchestra Layout

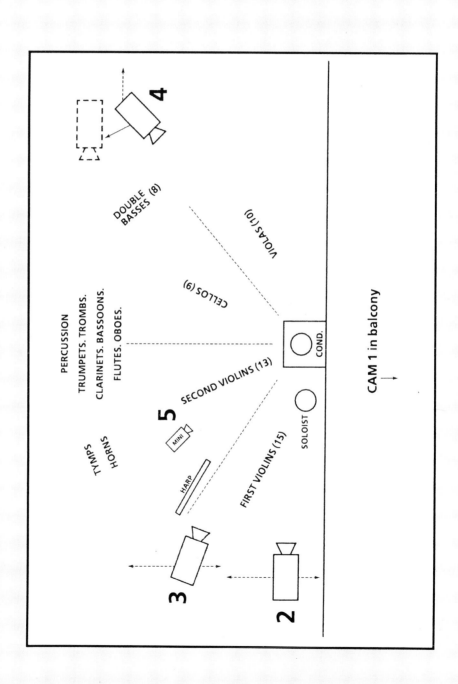

### Opera and ballet scripts

When you are working on an operatic piece, you have the stage directions and the words to help you keep your place.

A ballet script can take the form of a list of shot numbers and cameras with very detailed shot descriptions. When marking up your own script and during rehearsal, try to make a short note to help you recognise the shot. You won't have time to read the whole shot description. (See *Race-reading* on p.196 for further information).

If there is a clear storyline in the opera or ballet, type up a story or recording order similar to that used in drama, giving Act and Scene numbers, characters involved, time of day, cameras and shot numbers, plus a column for notes. Most of the production team will find this useful.

### Presenter's script

If you have a presenter, you will need to type the script for the introduction and links. At the beginning and end of each link, indicate which shot and item you are going to and from and then insert the relevant pages into your score or grid in the appropriate place.

### Copyright

Once your music has arrived, check to see if copyright is applicable by contacting a music copyright specialist or the publishing house shown on the music.

### Costing

If you haven't already done so, start keeping a costing book or section in your file. Apart from general costs, you might have to include music hire, music copyright, management fees, facility fees for the venue, including power and lights that you may use, cost of the seats that the hall will be unable to sell because of camera positions or cables, orchestra fees including porterage and doubling.

## Planning meetings

If the programme is of a musical performance the planning meeting is usually held at the venue. If it can't be, the technical co-ordinator and engineering manager will have to arrange their own meeting at the site.

The more meetings and recces that you can attend the better, especially if you are not familiar with the location. If all else fails arrange your own private visit attending another concert or event if necessary.

## Technical requirements

As with any outside broadcast, your producer or director will produce some technical requirements after the planning meeting. Get these and your notes down on paper as soon as possible, type them up and distribute them to those involved. Details of information required on technical requirements appears in Chapter 14 on p.145-7.

## Fitting in with the rehearsals

Check rehearsal times with the orchestral manager, agent or concert organiser and make sure they know how important it is that you know of any changes. Quite often you will only get very limited rehearsal and not have control over how many, what time or where. The production team will have to fit in with the orchestra's plans.

## Extra requirements

Remember to find out if you need to arrange a piano and piano stool, music stands and chairs, or conductor's rostrum. If you have a piano, then you must book a piano tuner. None of these things happen automatically.

## Instrument hire/security/insurance

Sometimes special period musical instruments have to be hired. There are specialist companies that will be able to help and advise you, but the instruments will be very valuable, and expensive to hire. You will also have to make arrangements for security while they are in your possession as well as taking out special insurance.

### Timings

As usual, time everything during rehearsal and recordings. Check that timings are given on the record you are practising with so that, even if you haven't met the musicians themselves, you'll have an idea of how long the piece might be. Time songs, scenes, acts, movements, or whatever seems the best way of dividing the music.

If your programme is a live transmission, then you will need to have a good idea of how long everything is going to run, including links, applause, encores and pauses. You will also need to back time the last movements or pieces of music so that you can give repeated indications of how much music is left until the end. From your information, presentation can then gauge if transmission schedules need to be adjusted with a live concert. The director might decide to drop an item or lengthen a link, based on your calculations.

As with all live programmes a time chart is essential here so that you can keep checking your maths and make comparisons (see Chapter 10, *Timings & Time Charts*). Lighting find it useful to know how long to the end of a piece of music, because they can then stand by to bring up house lights or know how long to their next cue. The stage manager or floor manager will also need to know for cueing the presenter.

### Re-takes

For a recording, note down time codes at the beginning and end of music or scenes, and any others that you can manage in between. Note the time codes for re-takes, mistakes or problems, so that these can be found quickly for editing. Make sure all problems have been covered by the re-takes and let the director know if you feel that something is still missing. Don't forget to note down the reason why the re-take is necessary.

## Previewing

Previewing cameras can be difficult if you are following a score of a difficult piece of music. With practice and experience, it becomes easier to glance up in the right direction as you call the next camera to check that the correct shot is being lined up.

## Bar counting

Most PAs have heard of bar counting, even if they haven't had to do any themselves, and many dread the moment. However, quite often it can turn out to be a very enjoyable experience. If you know that you have no sense of rhythm, then you will find it more difficult.

If you can tap time to a pop record with your foot, then the chances are you will be perfectly capable. Most pop music is written in 4/4 time: that is to say, there are four beats in a bar. You will find that counting 1,2,3,4 will seem to 'fit' the music very well. You will probably begin to count to the rhythm quite easily and naturally begin your '1' on the first beat of a bar. This is because there is an emphasis or stress on that first beat.

The whole point of bar counting is to indicate to the cameraman how quickly the shots are being taken, how long the shot is going to be held or how long for the zoom or pan.

Your first job is to get a copy of the lyrics and retype them with plenty of space. The director will then work out the shots he wishes to use with the song, marking in cut lines. Meanwhile, you can be listening to the music and practising counting in time. Having got the director's script, type up a neat version, putting in shot numbers.

This is where your hard work begins. By listening to the music and following the director's script or the words, you need to count the bars for each shot, and write down the number.

After each shot change, start from one again and count to the next shot change. For example, there may be four bars worth of shot 1, six bars for shot 2, 2 bars for shot 3 and 4 bars for shot 4 and so on. Your counting would be like this:

```
shot 1
-----------------------/
            1,2,3,4,
            2,2,3,4,
            3,2,3,4,
            4,2,3,4,

shot 2
-----------------------/
            1,2,3,4,
            2,2,3,4,
            3,2,3,4,
            4,2,3,4,
            5,2,3,4,
            6,2,3,4,

shot 3
-----------------------/
            1,2,3,4,
            2,2,3,4,

shot 4
-----------------------/
            1,2,3,4,
            2,2,3,4,
            3,2,3,4,
            4,2,3,4,
```

Having got to the end, run through the music and words again, to check that you still agree with your original count. Don't expect to get it right the first time, you may have to keep stopping and starting the tape as you run through this familiarisation process.

Once you have worked out the bars for each shot, type the number in brackets towards the end of each shot. On your own script, mark the number in big red figures or whatever method you wish to adopt.

Make sure that you can distinguish the bar numbers from the cameras and see them quickly and clearly on the script. You then type the camera cards putting down the shot number, description and the number of bars for each shot.

Whilst you are counting, however, you may discover that the cutting point does not always come neatly at the end of a bar. The cut may come half-way through a bar, in which case you end up with odd beats. For example, there may be three whole bars, plus the first two beats of the fourth bar and then the shot changes.

If this is the case, you will be counting:

> 1,2,3,4,
> 2,2,3,4,
> 3,2,3,4,
> 1,2,

Beats three and four of the fourth bar don't disappear, you just don't count them aloud. This is because you don't have time as on each and every shot change, you are also shot calling in the usual way giving the next camera. With practise, you can say all this during the first bar of the new shot.

As you get more experienced you will discover that you do not need to vocalise every beat to keep in time with the music, and if you did you would drive everyone else mad — so learn to count the beats under your breath. Anyway, there would be far too many numbers being called if you counted every beat and that would become confusing.

So, you need to call the shot (on the first beat of the first bar), then you need to tell the cameraman how long the shot is going to be. This is done within your count, (usually on the second beat of the first bar) by saying for example: "2 of 8" (for an eight bar shot), then count the rest of the beats under your breath, but vocalising each new bar.

If there are quite a few bars for one shot, it is useful to remind everyone how many bars you are counting to. So you could call "4 of 8" or "half-way", at the appropriate time, ending with "8 of 8", so the cameraman knows where he is at all times. If you find you do not have enough time to call the shots and count the bars, at least keep up with the shot numbers. If you really find bar counting impossible, although I promise you it comes with practice, follow the lyrics and announce the number of lines to the shot change.

One of the most difficult parts of bar counting is starting off. Quite often introductions are slow, have no rhythm or the tempo changes after the first few bars. If you find it difficult to bar count an opening, use a stopwatch to give you a timing to the first clear beat.

Practise with the music and the script as much as possible because when you come to bar counting with pictures as well, things become more difficult!

The cutting points may not always happen precisely as planned and you must not call the shot if it has not been cut up. The vision mixer is not cutting to your count all the time, as a camera may not be in position or a boom may be in shot.

If a shot is late, keep your planned count going quietly to yourself and then, when the shot appears, call the shot and pick up on the bar you have reached on the script. Don't try to adjust the number of bars because the shot has been shortened. If you get lost, don't count something and hope for the best — call the shots only or keep quiet until you can find your place.

Curiously, many of us seem to be self-conscious about moving our bodies in time to the music when it is for work and not the disco. Get some part of your body moving when bar counting, even if it is only your big toe under the desk, because your shot calling cannot keep to the rhythm all the time.

Some people 'conduct' with a pencil, others sway forwards and backwards in the chair. Do whatever you feel the most natural (within reason!) and ignore the fact that everyone else is sitting rigid. You won't have time to notice anyway.

## Counting backwards

Some directors want bars to be counted backwards, this is especially appropriate for brass bands where the shots can last as long as 32 or even 64 bars. This saves you saying "of however many bars" as you just keep counting back to zero which is the end of the shot.

## Race-reading

The term sounds very daunting but actually consists of 'reading' ahead and keeping everyone including, your director, informed as to what is about to happen. You may find yourself having to race-read in a situation where you have no script or score to follow and in some cases, not even the luxury of a rehearsal.

## Race-reading action

It is during the rehearsal that you need to make as many notes as you possibly can, describing the action or moves and then reading out those notes in advance of them happening.

As a result you will be talking virtually non-stop. For example, during a piece of modern dance or ice-skating you need to note down any dramatic leaps or movements and warn everyone what is about to happen so that the cameraman can move to a wide angle and the director will cut to that camera to accommodate the leap.

Nobody expects you to be technically accurate with your descriptions of leaps, but a rough description of the movement, with indications of where the dancers are coming from or going to is what is needed.

## Race-reading unscripted music

You may have the music for a jazz band but there has been no time for scripting the music. The music will be 'as directed' and you will be calling out which instrument is about to play next.

An example would be: the clarinet playing a slow introduction, the saxophone joining in, followed by the whole band for a few bars, then the piano playing the main theme. If you can, give the number of bars too. The director will be able to concentrate on looking at the shots, if you are looking ahead in the music and previewing the next instrument.

### Popular music

If a pop group is well known, then it may be difficult to arrange for it to come to the studio to appear on your programme. However, most pop groups jump at the chance as television is such good publicity.

### Pluggers

When dealing with pop groups and individual singers, the PA will have most contact with the record plugger from the record company concerned.

### Backing track

The group are generally given the option of performing live or miming to their original recording. Before they can be recorded, you need to find out from the record plugger the names of the vocalists on the backing track.

If these singers are foreign artists, then another track may have to be made with British vocalists before it can be used in the studio and transmitted. Quarter-inch tapes of the music need to be obtained from the record company to use in the studio.

### Editing

You will need to establish with the director the plans for editing, as this can affect the way you record your programme. Generally a main recording on VT is made, plus a backing copy. Quite often you will hear the word ISO mentioned. This simply means an isolated recording on a separate machine, some-times using a locked-off camera. This shot may be a general wide angle of the stage or of the conductor of the orchestra.

Having this additional recording gives you an alternative shot to use if you have a problem editing the main material.

### Sub-titles

You must also check whether sub-titles are being played in at the edit or if a character generator and operator will be needed for titles and end credits.

### Co-productions

If your production is a co-production, you may also have to make another version of the transmission tape according to the contract, so make sure you have booked enough time to allow for this.

If you have kept accurate time codes and thorough re-take notes from the recording, you will help to make the editing move quickly and efficiently.

### Sypher

As the sound is obviously very important on a music pro-gramme, you will frequently have to book sypher a few days after your editing dates. Your sound supervisor will advise you on whether sypher is necessary. If you have stereo recordings then it will certainly be required.


# BALLET

If you are recording the ballet on location, the costumes may be provided by the ballet company, but make sure everyone is happy with these for television close-ups. It is a good idea to book a costume designer or assistant to check details anyway. Similarly, dressers may be needed to give the clothes a quick iron if necessary and work with the company wardrobe person. The dancers may also do their own make-up, but you will need a television make-up artist to advise them for the camera.

The cost of television ballet is huge. NATTKE (National Association of Television Technicians and Kinematograph Employees) is the union that looks after all the back stage people and technicians. Generally there is a large payment to cover their assistance in putting the production on the television screen.

There is a negotiated all-in fee which should be dealt with by the artists booker or someone experienced in this field. Other fees are, of course, for the dancers themselves, the choreographer and sometimes the design copyright which can occasionally include costumes.

If the dance is being recorded in a television studio, then a special dance floor may have to be laid. This will be organised by your designer and there are companies that provide these.

Make sure you know when all the rehearsals are taking place and, with the permission of the ballet company, go to as many as possible. Find out if there are any performances of the ballet that you can also attend.

# OPERA

Much of the setting up for opera is similar to what has been discussed so far. As most opera on television will be a relay from an outside location, the most important job for the PA is liaison with the venue.

In addition you will, of course, have words to deal with, which may not be in English. Translations will have to be organised and arrangements made for sub-titles to appear on the screen, as close as possible to the moment the lyrics are sung and in a concise, but comprehensible, form.

The best way to store the sub-titles is on a floppy disc using time code which can then be recalled as the transmission spool is played.

## Speedy music checklist

- Get the score/lyrics
- Story line for ballet or opera
- Copyright checks
- Planning meeting
- Technical requirements
- Visit rehearsals
- Visit venue for performance
- Instrument hire and security insurance
- Bar counting
- Race reading
- Backing track recordings
- Co-productions
- Sub-titles

# WHERE DO YOU GO FROM HERE?

Is there life after being a PA? Well, in theory, the role of the PA should be the very best broad-based and most practical background experience anyone can have before moving up the production ladder. But if only life were that simple ....

Unfortunately, what tends to happen is that everyone keeps saying "but you're such a good PA, why do you want to do anything else?" Even if you are given the chance to move on up the production ladder, your PA role tends to stay with you and you can bet your boots someone will expect you to retain some of the duties of the PA instead of giving you the freedom to progress with your new job.

Some PAs feel they have no alternative but to move organisations in order to shake off the role. There are more and more production and facilities houses which require PAs for corporate videos, commercials and commissioned work. Cable and satellite channels are springing up all over the place needing good qualified PAs.

Or there is always the freelance route. If you are the sort who is prepared to tackle anything, slipping neatly into any company's way of doing things, this may be the future for you.

If you wish to spread your wings further, there is always the feature film industry in need of good organisers and continuity assistants.

One thing is certain, the role of the PA is so crucial to the industry that no good PA should have trouble finding work in the foreseeable future, whatever specialist field she chooses.

However, a fact of life is that many PAs feel the need for greater challenges and desire to move up the production ladder. But when they leave, it follows that new enthusiastic PAs are given the opportunity to begin their production careers. Good luck to them all — there are exciting times ahead!

# GLOSSARY

Television has created a considerable amount of technical shorthand and jargon. Nothing like all of it appears in this glossary — that would take a book in itself — nor do all the following terms appear in the text of this book, but the following is a small selection of some of the more common expressions you may come across as a PA.

**AB** or **A/B** As before.

**A-B rolls** **1.** Two telecine machines operating in sync so that mixes can be made from a separate control room. **2.** Two VT machines operating in sync so that mixes can be made either locally or in a remote control room. **3.** Two rolls of film or videotape containing alternate shots overlapping, to permit mixes of effects to be made on to a third roll.

**AFM** Assistant floor manager.

**acoustics** The science of sound.

**action** **1.** The physical content of a scene. **2.** The cue given by the director when film camera and sound are running at speed.

**action props** Objects which are handled by artists, as opposed to ornaments which dress the set.

**actuality** Real events, as opposed to reconstructed or fictional scenes.

**angle of view** The angle in the horizontal plane defining the limits of a scene.

**answer print** A complete colour print from the cut negative where the detailed grading and opticals have still to be accepted. A stage between the cutting copy and the show print. See **cutting print, show print**.

**anti-flare** Solution used to spray down glass or other surfaces which are too highly reflective.

**aperture** The opening in a diaphragm forming part of an optical system that determines the amount of light passing through a lens.

**Arri (Arriflex)** Film camera.

**artwork** Any two dimensional graphic material for use within a programme, e.g. illustrations, logos, diagrams, photographs, titles, credits, etc.

**aspect ratio** The ratio of the width of a picture to its height.

**atmos** Atmosphere (of sound). See **buzz track**, **wild track**.

**atmosphere** Background sound.

**autocue** A device mounted on a camera so that an artist/-contributor can read the script while looking at the lens.

**BCU** See **big close up**.

**B/G** or **b/g** See **background**.

**BITC** A frame-by-frame time display seen on videotape. Used for **logging** and **editing**.

**BP** See **back projection**.

**BVU** See **broadcast video U-matic**

**b/w** Black and white.

**backdrop** A scene painted on canvas to form the background to action.

**background (B/G or b/g)** That part of a scene which is farthest from the point of interest (in sound or vision).

**background camera** Term used in **chromakey (CSO)** for the camera viewing the material infilled as background to the subject on the foreground camera. See **colour separation overlay**.

**backing 1.** Element of scenery seen through an opening, e.g. a door window or arch. **2.** In music, a combination of instruments subordinate to the leads.

**backing copy** A duplicate videotape or film recording made as a reserve to the principal copy.

**backing track** A pre-recording used as an accompaniment to a live performance.

**back projection** Film or video projection on to the rear of the viewing screen.

**barn door** A framework of metal flaps fitted to the front of a lantern which can be adjusted to shape the beam.

**barrel** Hanging bar. See **lighting barrel**.

**Betacam** A half-inch gauge broadcast-quality video cassette.

**Betamax** A domestic video recording and playback system.

**big close up (BCU)** Frame filled with head, usually cutting above eyes and on chin.

**black edge generator** Puts a black edge round caption lettering.

**blocking** First rehearsal of a scene when movements are being set. Also used to describe the first camera rehearsal.

**boom** A telescopic arm for positioning a microphone.

**break up 1.** The disintegration of a television picture. **2.** Part of a set or a prop constructed to collapse as part of the action.

**brightness** The amount of light reflected by or produced by a surface per unit of area.

**broadcast video U-matic (BVU)** Broadcast-quality "high band" 3/4-inch gauge videotape format.

**buzz-track** An **atmos** sound track.

**cam L** Camera left

**cam R** Camera right

**COMMAG** See **combined magnetic**.

**COMOPT** See **combined optical**.

**CSO** See **colour separation overlay**.

**CU / CS** See **close-up**.

**call sheet** A location timetable provided by the **AFM**, containing call times for artists.

**camcorder** Video camera with built-in recorder.

**camera angle 1.** The camera's horizontal angle of view.
**2.** Loosely, a protractor showing lens acceptance angles.

**camera card** Cameraman's cue card showing an individual camera's shots according to the camera script.

**camera left** Left-hand side of the set from the cameraman's point of view.

**camera right** Right-hand side of the set from the cameraman's point of view.

**camera script** Script marked up with shot numbers, cutting points, cameras, lighting.

**camera tapes** (or **rushes**) The master videotapes shot on location, to be used later for the final 'on-line' edit. In film practice, rushes are the first prints made from the newly-processed negatives to check content and quality. Also referred to as **dailies** or **rush prints**.

**camera tower** Stock scaffolding tower for high-angle shots.

**camera trap** Opening frame (hinged or sliding) in a set for a camera to shoot through. Usually concealed to look like a picture, panelling, etc.

**cans** Headphones.

**caption card** Slightly outdated mode of graphics, used for mounting titles, credits, photographs, diagrams, etc.

**caption generator** Studio or editing suite-based word processor for storing and re-producing captions, supered over studio, VT or film. Also referred to as **cap gen** or **character generator**.

**caption scanner (slide scanner)** Video channel for electronic reproductions of pictures from 35mm transparencies.

**cheat** A legitimate deception to achieve a desired result, e.g. to cheat an eyeline.

**chromakey (CSO)** See **colour separation overlay**.

**clapperboard** Board used with film for scene and take numbering and syncing up with film sound.

**clear** 1. A cue, usually spoken, to any operator that a particular shot or action is complete. 2. To remove scenery, props, equipment, or artists.

**clip** A piece of film taken out of a sequence.

**clipping level** The threshold to which a clipper is set on the vision mixing desk, so that super-impositions cut through cleanly.

**close-up (CU)** Head and shoulders shot.

**colour balance** 1. Part of the line-up process of a colour camera. 2. The fine adjustments made to colour cameras during rehearsal, recording or transmission.

**colour bars** Eight vertical bars which appear on the screen as a test signal. From left to right, white, yellow, cyan, green, magenta, red, blue, black.

**colour grading** Scene-by-scene adjustment of colour intensities in film printing or video transfer recording.

**colour separation overlay** A device used, so that when shooting a scene against a background of a given colour, an electronic switch will enable another source to be overlaid into the background or infill foreground. Electronic equivalent of travelling matte in film.

**combined magnetic** (COMMAG) Picture film with combined magnetic stipe for sound.

**combined optical** (COMOPT) Picture film with combined optical track for sound.

**complementary angle** One shot taken to match another in a two-handed sequence.

**conform** The editing of a programme or sequence on a high quality format to match a low quality, bold off-line edit.

**continuity** The record kept of all action in non-continuous shooting so that shots will cut together correctly, e.g. position of artists, furniture, hand props, camera angles, lens heights, lighting levels, costumes and make-up.

**control line** A telephone line providing communication between two areas for technical or production purposes.

**control track** Signal recorded on a videotape to control the machine during replay.

**cross cut** To cut alternately from one shot to another or from one scene to another so that sections of each are seen successively. Also **intercut**.

**crossing the line** A fault in direction which occurs when a scene is shot from two opposite sides so that the characters appear to keep reversing their position in relation to each other when the pictures are cut together.

**cut-away** Separate shots taken after the main action, to provide detail or illustration for an interview.

**cut throat** Signal given to a speaker to indicate that he must draw his speech or item to an immediate close.

**cutting copy** The first positive edited film (includes editor's cutting marks, joins, etc.). See **cutting print**, **rough cut**, **show print**.

**cutting print** The particular positive print which the editor assembles and on which he works.

**cyc (cyclorama)** A large neutral backing formed by stretching a plain-coloured cloth horizontally and vertically around two or three sides of a studio.

**cyc track** Permanent rail with movable runners to which a cyc can be attached.

**D** or **D/S** See **downstage**.
**D.E.L.** See **direct exchange line**.
**dead 1.** Non-reverberant.
**2.** Scenery, props or equipment that is finished with.

**defocus** To blur an image electronically or optically.

**depress** To decrease a camera's lens height.

**depth of field** Measure of the distance between the nearest and farthest point at which the image is in focus.

**dialogue** The spoken words in both scripted or unscripted programmes.

**direct exchange line** An external telephone line provided in an outside broadcast scanner.

**dissolve (or mix)** A transition between two images or sounds whereby one gradually disappears and is replaced by another.

**disk** A gramophone record.

**downstage (D/S)** The section of the acting area nearest to the audience or camera.

**dress run** Dress or final rehearsal before shooting/performance.

**dressing** The furniture, ornaments, pictures, etc which establish the period and character of a set.

**dropout** Brief loss of signal causing picture disturbance on videotape.

**drop-shadow** An edge added to supered caption, putting the caption into relief.

**dry** To forget a line or word of dialogue.

**dry run** Run-through of a show without all practical props, effects and/or cameras and sound.

**dub 1.** To transfer recorded sound or to record. Hence dubbing: the action of re-recording and by extension the preparation of composite sound track from several ingredients such as commentary, music, dialogue and effects all recorded on separate tracks laid for dubbing. **2.** To re-record the sound track of a film, substituting for the original speech, a spoken translation in another language.

**dubbing mixer** The sound recordist who controls the sound mixing panel in the dubbing theatre and is responsible for the final sound track mixed from other tracks, disk or live sound.

**dubbing sheets** Information on the exact position of all sound on the final mixed track provided by the film editor or the dubbing mixer.

**dubbing suite or theatre** A set of rooms containing all the equipment used in dubbing.

**dupe** Duplicate.

**duplicate negative (dupe neg)** A negative made from the master.


**ENG** See **electronic news gathering.**

**ELS** See **extreme long shot.**

**ext** Exterior.

**editing** The process of joining the film or videotape footage to compile an item or whole programme.

**edit pair** Two adjacent VT machines equipped for electronic editing.

**edit suite** Three adjacent VT machines equipped for more elaborate editing including mixes and electronic effects.

**effects (F/X)** Sound or visual material added to a scene to create atmosphere either as a background or specific, e.g. traffic noise or fire flicker.

**effects box (F/X box)** A box containing bells, buzzers, etc. for offstage effects.

**effects track** Sound track of sound effects other than speech and music.

**electronic news gathering (ENG)** Lightweight portable camera kit with crew.

**elevate** To increase a camera's lens height.

**establishing shot** The first shot which shows the geography of a set or location.

**extreme long shot (ELS)** A panoramic shot in which individuals cannot be identified.

**eyeline** The direction in which an artist is looking.


**FAV** See **favour.**

**F/G** or **f/g** See **foreground.**

**FPS 1.** Feet per second.
**2.** Frames per second.

**F/X** Effects.

**F/X box** See **effects box.**

**facilities** The provision of technical equipment and crews for any stage of production.

**fade** To increase or decrease gradually the volume of sound or the brightness of picture. So **fade in, fade out, fade up, fade down.**

**fader** Device for fading sound, vision or lighting.

**favour (FAV)** To give prominence to any part of a picture.

**film insert** Filmed material inserted into an electronic television programme.

**film recording** The transfer of an electronic video signal on to film.

**final run** Last rehearsal before transmission or recording.

**fire lane** Line on studio floor marking the limits of usable space and the width of a clear passage between it and the studio wall.

**fish eye lens** An extreme wide angle lens giving an effect similar to a convex mirror.

**fishing rod** Hand-held microphone boom.

**flag** A rectangular card or piece of wood on a stand used to mask light from camera lens or object.

**flare** Usually detrimental effect from a lamp shining into a lens or reflected from a bright surface into a lens.

**flash back** A scene depicting past events.

**flat** A completely flat piece of scenery made in different widths and heights. May include architectural features. Hence arch flat, door flat, double door flat.

**flat lighting** Lighting without prominent keylight, resulting in a lack of shadow or depth on a set.

**flood** A soft source of light.

**floor marks** Chalk or tape marks on studio floor to show correct position for artists, scenery, props, cameras or booms.

**floor painting** Colours or patterns painted on to the studio floor.

**floor plan** Plan of a TV or film studio showing the disposition of sets, furniture, audience seating and equipment.

**fluff** To speak a word or line of dialogue incorrectly or hesitantly.

**foldback** A sound signal fed to a loudspeaker on the studio floor from the sound control room.

**footage 1.** Length of film expressed in feet. **2.** Collection of related film sequences.

**footage counter** Mechanically or electronically operated display showing length of film.

**foreground (F/G or f/g)** The part of a scene that is nearest the audience or camera (in sound or vision).

**format** Different videotape systems, e.g. **1", Betacam, U-matic, VHS**, etc. Videotape of a given format can only be played back on a corresponding machine.

**fount** (typeface) A given style of alphanumeric characters available for selection on a character generator.

**frame 1.** A single photographic shot in cinefilm or electronic camera. **2.** To construct a picture in which the essential elements are kept within the picture limits.

**freeze frame** A single frame which is held to give the effect of freezing the action.

**fringing** The appearance of spurious edges of incorrect colour at the margins of coloured areas.

**gaffer** The head electrician on a unit.

**gallery** Studio control room.

**gauge** The measure applied to cine film which specifies the standard, i.e. the overall width, size and spacing of sprocket holes, size of picture, sound strip, etc.

**generation** The original version of a tape or film is the master or first generation. Further copies, made either by duplication or by editing, become second, third, etc.

**genlock** The means by which a remote television source may be made synchronous at a studio mixer for superimposition or split-screen working. The signals from the remote pulse generator are made to steer the master pulse generator. If several remote sources, only one can be so used at a time. Now largely obsolete.

**ghosting** Apparent repetition of an image on the screen.

**grading** The process of matching the colour balance between filmed scenes by altering the colour of the printer light during printing.

**grams** Record or disc-playing equipment.

**grey scale** A test card, showing graded steps from white to black, used during line-up of colour cameras.

**grips** Film assistant responsible for transporting and operating heavy camera equipment, e.g. dollies.

**ground row** The name given to the lamps which light a cyclorama or backcloth.

**guide track 1.** Sound track recorded during shooting to serve as a guide for post-synchronisation and not for use in the finished programme. **2.** Sound track specially pre-recorded to keep an artist or an orchestra in synchronism with accompanying pictures. Also **playback track**.

**H/A** High angle.

**headroom** The space on the screen between the top of a performer's head and the upper edge of the picture.

**headlamp** Lantern mounted on camera.

**headset** Headphones with microphone attached.

**helical scan** A type of videotape machine where the vision is recorded in long slanting tracks across the tape.

**high-band** A generic term for the **BVU format** which also provides a low-band system which is of inferior quality. See **BVU** and **format**.

**house lights** Working lights in studio.

**int** Interior.

**insert** A short item or sequence inserted into a programme and forming part of it.

**intercut** To cut between two shots or scenes to direct the audience's attention in a particular way.

**iris** The variable aperture of a lens which controls the amount of light falling on the film or camera receptor.

**iso** Isolated camera feed, recorded separately to cover certain action to help with editing.

**jack** Type of plug used to carry sound signals.

**jack field** Multiple rows of jack sockets.

**jelly** A gelatine diffuser, coloured, transparent, or translucent, for fitting into the front of a light source.

**jib** The arm of a camera crane.

**join** See **splice**.

**jump cut** A cut which, by accident or design, does not follow a smooth continuity and so produces a shock effect.

**key light** The primary light giving shape and form to any object.

**keying colour** Colour selected for the operation of **CSO**.

**kill** To remove from set if unwanted.

**L** Camera left.

**L/A** Low angle.

**LS** See **long shot**.

**leader** A standard initial length of film or videotape to allow the reproducing machinery time to run up to the correct speed, i.e. picture stabilisation and pitch of sound.

**lighting barrel** A suspended bar from which lanterns are hung.

**lighting cameraman** Another term for film cameraman, as he is responsible for lighting locations, as well as operating the camera.

**lighting console** Electronic equipment for remotely controlling the brightness of individual or groups of lamps.

**lighting hoist** Remote control machinery for suspended lighting barrels.

**lighting plot** A plan of the lighting rig prepared in advance.

**lighting rig** The number of lanterns and their disposition.

**line standard** The number of lines in a TV picture, e.g. 625 in the UK, 525 in USA.

**line up** Action of preparing electronic equipment to a specific standard.

**lip microphone** A mic designed to be held very close to the speaker's mouth.

**lip sync** Where lip movement and the speech heard are simultaneous.

**live** Action simultaneously broadcast.

**location shot** A shot taken anywhere remote from the studio.

**lock** To be in **sync**. See **genlock**.

**logging** Noting studio or location recorded material required for editing.

**long shot (LS)** A full length shot of the human body.

**loop** A length of tape or film joined to form an endless loop providing the recorded effect continuously.

**lot** Space outside film studio where exterior sets can be built.

**M & E track** Music and effects track.

**MCPS** See **Mechanical Copyright Protection Society**.

**MCR** Mobile control room.

**MCU** See **medium close-up**.

**MLS** See **medium long-shot**.

**MS** See **medium** (or mid) **shot**.

**magazine** Container for film in camera and projector.

**magnetic track** Sound track on which the sound is recorded magnetically.

**master neg** The original negative film used in the camera. Usually a dupe is used for printing purposes to avoid the possibility of damaging the original.

**master tape** Usually final edited version for transmission. Sometimes applied to an original tape.

**matte** A mask whose position, shape and dimensions determine the area of the image seen. Used in film and **CSO**. See **colour separation overlay, travelling matte**.

**Mechanical Copyright Protection Society (MCPS)** receives payments for all recorded music used in a programme. See **PRS**.

**medium close up** A shot normally of the head and shoulders, used mostly in interviews.

**medium long shot** A shot which cuts below the knee.

**medium (or mid) shot (MS)** between a **close-up (CU)** and a **long shot (LS)**. For instance, a human subject framed from the waist upwards is said to be in a medium shot.

**mic** Microphone.

**mirror shot** Where the camera sees reflections of people or objects in a mirror.

**mix** Overlapping transition between one picture and another.

**mixer** The apparatus which enables the outputs of either sound or vision channels to be faded up and down.

**mole crane** Three-man operated camera mounting with counter- balanced jib arm.

**monitor** A television screen fed by pictures from cameras, **VT** or **TK**.

**monochrome** MONO (single) CHROMinance (colour). Generally used as an alternative for **black and white**.

**montage** A sequence of quick cuts, mixes, etc. Used to encapsulate varied action over a long period of time or for dream sequences.

**mute** Film without sound.

**N/A** See **narrow angle**.

**NTSC** See **National Television Systems Committee**.

**narrow angle (N/A)** Camera angle expressed in degrees; the lower the number the narrower the angle.

**National Television Systems Committee (NTSC)** The colour television system used mainly in the USA, Canada and Japan. Colour information is transmitted according to the phase and amplitude of a carrier wave.

**noise 1.** Appears as snow on the TV screen . **2.** Sound — b/g hiss.

**OB** Outside broadcast.

**OOV** Out of vision.

**O/R** Outside rehearsal.

**O/S** Over shoulder shot.

**off-line** The VT version of **rough cut**. An edit performed on an inexpensive (non-broadcast)

format. This is subsequently **conformed** using the trans-mission format.

**on-line** Edit on to final format for transmission.

**one inch (1")** A broadcast-quality videotape format with one-inch- wide videotape carried on a reel rather than in a cassette casing.

**opt out** Fixed point in a network programme, where certain regions leave the national programme to continue regionally.

**optical 1.** Of any effect produced on film by means of an optical printer. **Optical mix. Optical fade. 2.** The effect so produced.

**overcranking** To run a film camera faster than normal to give a slow motion effect when projected.

**overlay** See **CSO**.

**PA 1.** Public address system. **2.** Production assistant.

**PAL** See **Phase Alternate Line**.

**PBU** See **photo blow-up**.

**PM** Production manager.

**POV** Point of view.

**PRS** See **Performing Rights Society**.

**pan** To rotate a camera through a horizontal arc. So **pan right, pan left, pan up, pan down.** Abbreviation from **panoramic**.

**panning handle** Extension to camera head by which cameraman controls camera movement.

**pass** Refers to the number of VT recordings made in a VT build-up. Pass is derived from the number of times the programme material passes the recording head. So **4-pass VT, 5-pass VT.**

**pedestal** Camera mounting.

**Performing Rights Society (PRS)** Receives payments for all composers and performers of music used in a programme. See **MCPS**.

**Phase Alternate Line (PAL)** The colour television system used in much of Western Europe.

**photo blow-up (PBU)** A photographic enlargement, often for a backing.

**post dub** To record additional material on the original sound track.

**post-synchronise** To record sound, e.g. dialogue or music, separately from picture and add the sound after the picture has been shot.

**practical** A prop or effect which is functional, i.e. table lamp, water tap, gas stove, piano, etc.

**pre-hear** A checking facility to ensure that a sound fader is being correctly fed.

**pre-record** To record part of a programme before the main programme.

**presentation** Continuity between broadcast programmes.

**preview 1.** To view a television picture before selecting it for transmission or recording. **2.** An advance showing of a film or videotaped programme.

**property (prop)** Any movable object used to dress a set or as part of the action. See **action prop**.

**pull focus** The action of altering focus on a television or film camera from one object to another as the point of interest changes.

**quadruplex machines (quad)** Type of videotape machine with four vision heads using two-inch (50mm) tape.

**R** Camera right.

**recce (reconnaissance or reconnoitre)** The survey made **1.** To choose a location and find what facilities it offers. **2.** To determine camera positions, lights needed, etc.

**record run (rec run)** Time code identifying the running time of a tape.

**recording break** An interruption to the recording process planned or inadvertent.

**retake 1.** To re-shoot a scene, a shot or sequence of shots. **2.** Name describing takes from Take 2 onwards.

**reversal film** Stock that is positive when processed. There is no negative.

**reverse angle** Shot complementary to the previous shot.

**reverse talkback** Talkback circuit, destination to source, i.e. OB to studio.

**roll-back and mix** A method of producing a mix between successive recorded sequences. The outgoing shot is replayed through the studio mixer and so mixed with the following live action or incoming shot from another VT machine.

**roller caption** A caption printed on a long strip of material which is wound in front of a camera from one to the other of two parallel rollers so that the caption appears to traverse the screen horizontally or vertically.

**rostrum (plural rostra)** An animation bench for film caption/model work.

**rostrum camera** Camera and mounting used to film static objects, e.g. pictures, maps with controlled zoom, and tracking and panning for frame-by-frame shooting.

**rough cut** The first assembly of portions of film in approximately the correct sequence to the final length.

**rubber numbers** Rubber numbers stamped on the side of both film and sound mag track prior to editing.

**run through** A rehearsal of the complete show.

**running time** Duration of production.

**rushes 1.** Rush prints; the first film prints of the day's shooting processed overnight. **2.** The process of viewing these rushes.

**SECAM** See **sequence couleur avec memoirs.**

**SEPMAG** Programme sound recorded on SEParate MAGnetic material.

**SEPOPT** Programme sound on SEParate OPTical film track.

**SOF** Sound on film.

**scanner** Another term for outside broadcast mobile control room.

**scene dock** Area used for storing scenery.

**schedule** A detailed timetable for location work. See **call sheet.**

**sequence** Part of a scene or of a whole programme.

**sequence couleur avec memoirs (SECAM)** Colour television system used in several countries, mainly France and USSR. The blue and red colour difference signals are transmitted on alternate television lines. One is displayed with the other by the artifice of a delay in the receiver.

**set-up** A particular camera position.

**shoot** The action of recording pictures on location.

**shooting script** Location script, including shots. See **shot list.**

**shot** One image offered by TV or film camera containing continuous action.

**shot list** A list of all the shots recorded on location. See **shooting script.**

**shot number** The sequential number given to each shot in a series for identification.

**show print** The final print for transmission in which all the grading is acceptable. See **cutting copy, cutting print, rough cut.**

**sixteen millimetre (16mm)** Standard documentary film gauge.

**slate** The scene number, e.g. Slate 72, Take 3.

**slide** A photographic transparency.

**slide scanner** Produces television pictures from 35mm transparencies.

**splice** A film join.

**split focus** To focus on a point between two objects widely spaced in depth from the camera, giving equal definition to both.

**split-screen** A picture in which two individually photographed elements appear separated by an optical edge. If more than two images are combined, the effect is known as **multiscreen.**

**spool 1.** The reel on which film or tape is wound. **2.** To wind tape or film from one spool to another.

**spot effects** Practical sound effects created live during a performance.

**standard converter** A device that converts programme material (live or recorded) from one television standard to another. This will however result in the loss of some picture quality.

**star filter** A filter placed in a camera to produce star-like radiations from highlights.

**Steenbeck** Trade name of a manufacturer, which has become a generic term for a film editing table.

**still** Photographs or visuals.

**stock** Film (moving or still) before it has been processed.

**storyboard** Drawings of a sequence of shots to indicate the visual content of a show.

**strike** To dismantle and remove sets and/or props.

**superimposition (super)** The placing of one image on top of another, so that both are simultaneously visible and appear through one another.

**sync** Synchronous.

**sync sound** Sound recorded simultaneously with the pictures.

**sypher (synchronous post helical scan eight-track recording)**. A system for upgrading and dubbing VT sound, by lifting sound off main VT, transferring it to multi-track tape recorder, re-mixing sound and relaying it back on to original VT.

**TK** Telecine.

**TX** Transmission.

**take 1**. To shoot a shot or a sequence of shots. **2.** The resulting shot/shots hence, Take 1, Take 2, etc.

**talkback** Audio communication via open microphone to one or more destinations, e.g. OB production talkback, studio production talkback, videotape talkback. The term switched is added if the microphone is switched at source, e.g. studio production, switched talkback.

**tarif (technical apparatus for the rectification of indifferent film)** Allows colour errors in a film to be corrected electronically in a telecine machine.

**tease** A brief mention at the top of a programme indicating items to follow later.

**technical run** Run-through of complete production at outside rehearsal specifically for the technicians responsible for lighting, sound, cameras, etc.

**telecine** An apparatus for generating television pictures from motion picture film.

**test card** Caption specially designed to convey the full range of monochrome and colour information for lining-up receivers.

**thirty-five millimetre (35mm)**: Standard film gauge for feature films and commercials.

**tilt (up and down)** To tip the camera through a vertical arc.

**time code** An electronic signal which can be recorded on to a tape to provide unique identification of frames or accurate timing information. See **time of day, record run**.

**time of the day** Time code showing actual time when shots were recorded.

**tone** Name given to the signal used for sound line-up of level.

**track** In or out, forward or backward movement of camera.

**track laying** To synchronise different sound sources for mixing to a master track.

**tracking line** The imaginary line on which a camera moves.

**trailer** A short sequence made for advertising a future programme.

**transfer** To re-record sound or vision from one standard to another, or from one system to another, that is, from film or videotape.

**trim** Unused remnants of film shots after editing.

**tripod** Camera mounting for film, electronic or still camera. Can have a panning and tilting head.

**U or U/S** See **up-stage**.

**U-matic** Video format using 3/4-inch tape. See **BVU, high-band, low-band**.

**under crank** To run a film camera at a slower than normal rate, this gives the effect of faster than normal movement when shown at normal speed or can be used to increase exposure on a static scene.

**under-run** To fall short of the planned duration.

**understudy** An actor who is rehearsed to replace another for a performance.

**up-stage (U or U/S)** Section of the acting area furthest from audience or camera.

**VHS** See **Video Home System**.

**VLS** Very long shot.

**VO** See **voice over**.

**VT** Videotape.

**VT clock** Videotape leader for accurate cueing of VT replays in the form of a clock which also shows programme identification number.

**VTR** See **videotape recording**.

**Video Home System (VHS)** Half-inch videotape cassette format most common in UK for domestic and office applications.

**videotape recording (VTR)** Recording on magnetic tape of vision signals with or without accompanying sound.

**viewfinder** 1. Display of camera output defining limits of frame, normally attached to camera. 2. Portable optical device with similar function.

**vignette** A masking frame of any shape placed in front of the camera lens to conceal part of a scene, e.g. keyhole effect.

**vision mixer** 1. The mixing panel. 2. The operator.

**voice over (VO)** Commentary over studio or location shots.

**W/A** Wide angle.

**WS** See **wide shot**.

**whip pan** To pan very rapidly.

**white balance** A means of setting colours and tones on a location video camera. Set by pointing the camera full frame on something peak white.

**wide shot (WS)** Includes whole set or large section of a scene.

**wild track** Sound track recorded independently of any picture with which it may subsequently be combined.

**wipe** Optical or electronic transition between two pictures employing a moving edge, hard, soft, horizontal, vertical, etc.

**X** Cross(es). Hence XC = crosses to centre (stage); XD, XU = crosses down/up (stage); XDC = crosses down centre; XL, XR = crosses to camera left/right; X/F = cross fade.

**Y** Symbol for luminance component of a television signal.

**zero dates** Fixed points in the run up to transmission when facilities have to be booked or stages in the production have to be completed.

**zoom** Lens with a continuously variable angle of view over a defined range, e.g. 5–50 degrees.

# Recommended Reading

*Continuity Notes* by Roger Singleton-Turner and Gill Partridge

*Shooting on Location* by Peter Jarvis

*Stand By Studio!* by Brian Phillips

*From Script to Screen* by Gordon Croton

*The Television Researcher's Guide* by Kathy Chater

All these titles are published by BBC Television Training